DRAGO

CW01465718

Copyright 2023 by Laurie Thurlow

Considerable effort has been taken to curate this collection. The author assumes no liability for any errors, omissions, or inaccuracies that may be present in this book.

Dedication

This book has been a work of love during a time of flux in my own life, where self-reflection and inward critical analysis has a critical part of my personal growth.

However, essential and enabling self-reflection is, it also allows you take stock of the greatest assets in your own life of which I have many. But it would be remiss of me not to mention and dedicate this work to two of these treasures:

Alison my ever-loving wife and life partner, who gives me cause to marvel at her wonderfulness on a daily basis.

Jody my daughter of whom a father could not be more proud, she is the jewel in my crown.

To these two beautiful women I owe so much, I hope they know the love I feel.

Forward:

In a world that often seems to move at an ever-increasing pace, finding moments of stillness and clarity can be challenging. As the constant waves of life crash around us, it becomes essential to anchor ourselves, to seek inner peace and balance amidst the chaos. In this pursuit, the power of mindfulness and the wisdom of inspirational quotes can act as beacons of light, guiding us toward a deeper understanding of ourselves and the world around us.

Welcome to this collection of inspirational quotes and mindfulness practices—a sanctuary of thought-provoking insights and timeless wisdom. Within these pages, you will embark on a transformative journey of self-discovery, reflection, and growth. Here, we invite you to pause, breathe, and open your heart to the messages that lie within each carefully curated quote.

In today's fast-paced society, it is all too easy to become lost in the hustle and bustle, to overlook the beauty that surrounds us, and neglect the treasures hidden within our own hearts. This book seeks to remedy that, offering a respite from the tumultuous world outside and inviting you to embark on a journey inward. By fostering a sense of mindfulness, we can reconnect with the present moment, cultivating awareness of our thoughts, feelings, and actions. Mindfulness is not just a practice; it is a way of life—a gateway to unlocking the limitless potential that resides within us.

The collection of inspirational quotes assembled here draws from the wisdom of sages, philosophers, poets, and visionaries from various cultures and eras. Each quote is like a pearl—a timeless gem that encapsulates profound truths and insights about life, love, resilience, and the human spirit. As you read and reflect on these words, you will find sparks of inspiration that resonate with your soul, empowering you to embrace life's challenges with courage, compassion, and grace.

Mindfulness and inspirational quotes complement each other beautifully. While mindfulness helps us live in the present moment and appreciate the journey, the quotes provide us with profound wisdom that nourishes our minds and hearts. Together, they offer a powerful and transformative force—one that can lead us to live with purpose, intention, and authenticity.

As you immerse yourself in the words of this book, remember that your journey toward mindfulness and self-discovery is unique and deeply personal. Embrace these pages with an open mind and heart, knowing that within each quote and mindfulness practice, there lies an opportunity for growth, healing, and profound transformation.

May this collection serve as a gentle reminder to cherish each moment, to find joy in the little things, and to embrace the challenges that come your way. May it inspire you to live with intention, kindness, and a sense of wonder. And most importantly, may it guide you to the realization that within you, there is an infinite reservoir of strength and wisdom waiting to be unveiled.

In the words of the great philosopher Lao Tzu, "The journey of a thousand miles begins with a single step." Let this book be that first step, guiding you towards a life of mindfulness and inspiring you to walk the path of authenticity and purpose.

With heartfelt gratitude for joining us on this voyage of inspiration and mindfulness.

What follows are 365 (1 for each day of the year) inspirational quotes with added explanation for personal growth and mindfulness.

Read, enjoy and grow

Laurie Thurlow

July 2023

Index

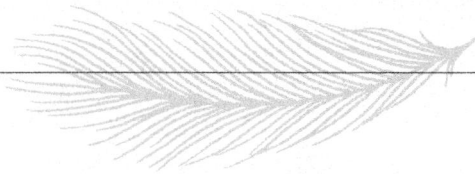

January 1st

"Your mind is a garden. Cultivate positive thoughts and watch your life bloom."

- The quote highlights the power of our thoughts in shaping our lives. Just as a garden needs nurturing and care, our minds require conscious effort to cultivate positive thinking and create a fulfilling life.

January 2nd

"Embrace change, for it is the essence of growth and transformation."

- Change is inevitable, and rather than resisting it, embracing change allows us to evolve and reach our true potential. Change provides us with opportunities for growth and helps us break free from limiting patterns.

January 3rd

"Practice gratitude daily, and watch your world expand with abundance."

- Gratitude is a powerful practice that shifts our focus from scarcity to abundance. By acknowledging and appreciating the blessings in our lives, we open ourselves up to receive more.

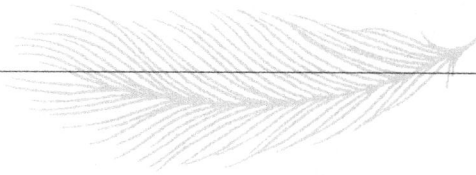

January 4th

"Be present in this moment, for it is all you truly have."

- The present moment is the only reality we have. By cultivating mindfulness and being fully present, we can experience life more deeply and engage with it in a meaningful way.

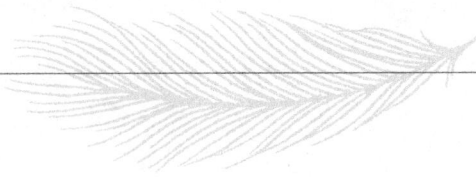

January 5th

"Let go of what no longer serves you to make space for what nourishes your soul."

- Holding onto things, relationships, or beliefs that no longer serve us hinders our personal growth. By letting go, we create space for new opportunities and experiences that align with our authentic selves.

January 6th

"Embrace failure as a stepping stone toward success and personal growth."

- Failure is not a setback but a lesson on the path to success. By reframing failure as an opportunity for growth, we can learn from our mistakes and improve ourselves.

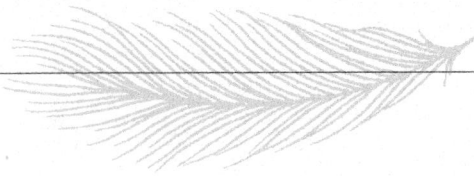

January 7th

"Your self-worth is not defined by others' opinions. It resides within you."

- Our self-worth should not be dependent on external validation. True self-worth comes from recognizing our inherent value and embracing our unique qualities.

January 8th

"In the face of adversity, find strength within yourself to rise above."

- Adversity is a part of life, but it doesn't define us. By tapping into our inner strength and resilience, we can overcome challenges and grow stronger in the process.

January 9th

"Be kind to yourself, for you are a work in progress."

- Self-compassion is essential on the journey of personal growth. Treat yourself with kindness and understanding, embracing the imperfections and acknowledging that growth takes time.

January 10th

"Choose love over fear, and watch your life transform."

- Love is a powerful force that can conquer fear. By cultivating love in our thoughts, actions, and relationships, we create a positive ripple effect that transforms our lives.

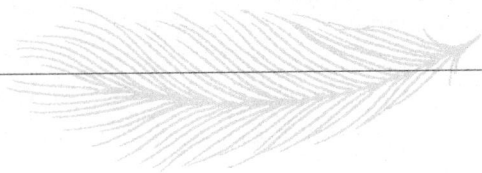

January 11th

"Forgiveness liberates the heart and frees the soul."

- Holding onto grudges and resentment only weighs us down. By practicing forgiveness, we release ourselves from the burden of the past and open ourselves up to healing and growth.

January 12th

"Seek knowledge, for it is the key that unlocks the doors of possibility."

- Lifelong learning is vital for personal growth. By actively seeking knowledge, we expand our perspectives, develop new skills, and open ourselves to a world of possibilities.

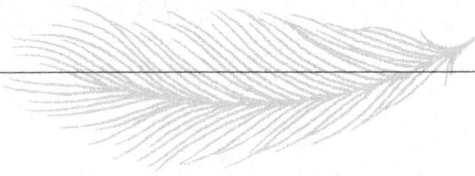

January 13th

"Embrace uncertainty, for within it lies the realm of infinite potential."

- Uncertainty can be unsettling, but it also holds tremendous opportunities for growth and discovery. Embracing uncertainty allows us to step out of our comfort zones and explore new horizons.

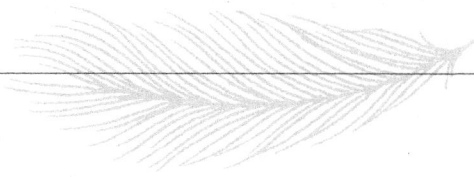

January 14th

"Your thoughts shape your reality. Choose them wisely."

- Our thoughts have the power to create our reality. By consciously choosing positive, empowering thoughts, we shape a more positive and fulfilling life experience.

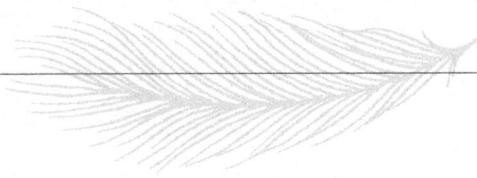

January 15th

"Practice self-care as a sacred ritual of honouring your mind, body, and soul."

- Self-care is essential for maintaining overall well-being. By prioritizing self-care and viewing it as a sacred ritual, we nurture our mind, body, and soul, allowing us to thrive.

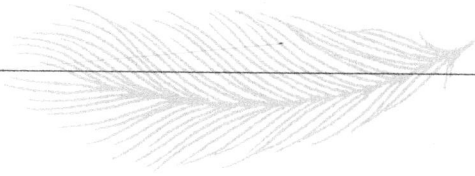

January 16th

"Every ending is a new beginning. Embrace the cycles of life."

- Life is a series of cycles, and every ending marks the start of something new. Embracing these cycles allows us to flow with life's natural rhythm and adapt to change more gracefully.

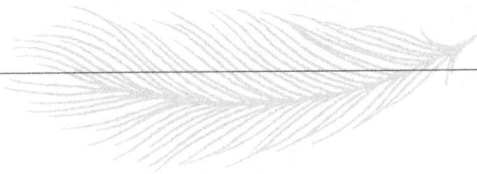

January 17th

"Release the need for perfection and embrace the beauty of your imperfections."

– Perfection is an unattainable ideal that can hinder personal growth. Embracing our imperfections allows us to celebrate our uniqueness and learn from our mistakes.

January 18th

"Your true strength lies in vulnerability. Dare to be authentically you."

– Vulnerability is not a weakness but a source of strength. By embracing vulnerability and showing up authentically, we invite deeper connections and foster personal growth.

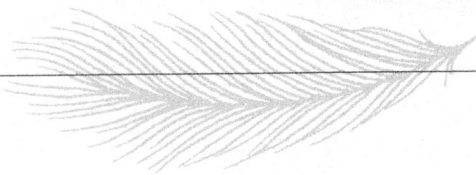

January 19th

"Nurture your passions and allow them to guide you on the path to fulfilment."

- Our passions are guiding lights that lead us to a life of purpose and fulfilment. By nurturing our passions and pursuing them with dedication, we create a life aligned with our true selves.

January 20th

"Let go of comparison and focus on your own journey."

- Comparison robs us of joy and hinders personal growth. By shifting our focus inward and embracing our own unique path, we can fully appreciate our own progress and achievements.

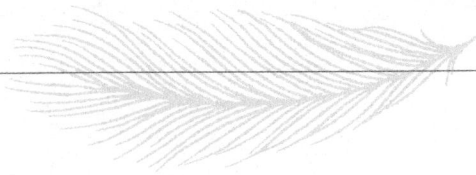

January 21st

"Practice self-reflection to gain insight and foster personal growth."

- Self-reflection is a powerful tool for self-awareness and personal growth. By taking time to reflect on our thoughts, actions, and experiences, we gain valuable insights that propel us forward.

January 22nd

"Embrace discomfort, for it is a catalyst for growth."

- Growth often occurs outside our comfort zones. By embracing discomfort and stepping into the unknown, we challenge ourselves, expand our boundaries, and unlock new levels of personal growth.

January 23rd

"Choose gratitude over complaint and watch your perspective shift."

- Gratitude transforms our perception. By shifting our focus from complaints to gratitude, we cultivate a positive mindset and invite more blessings into our lives.

January 24th

"Find balance in all aspects of your life to foster well-being and harmony."

- Balance is key to overall well-being. By seeking equilibrium in areas such as work, relationships, and self-care, we create a harmonious and fulfilling life.

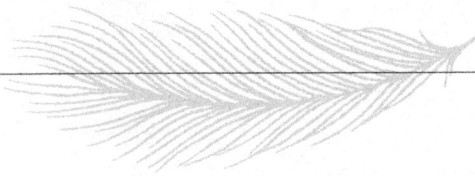

January 25th

"Practice deep listening and open yourself up to understanding others."

- Deep listening is a powerful practice that fosters connection and understanding. By fully engaging with others, we honour their perspectives and cultivate empathy and compassion.

January 26th

"Your journey is unique. Trust the timing of your life."

- Each person's journey unfolds at its own pace. Trusting the timing of your life allows you to let go of comparison and embrace the divine flow of your own path.

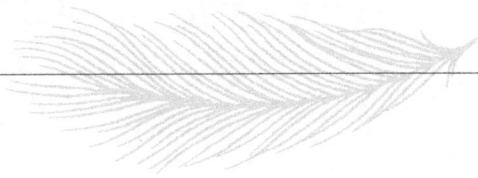

January 27th

"Embrace solitude as an opportunity for self-discovery and inner growth."

- Solitude provides a sacred space for self-reflection and introspection. By embracing moments of solitude, we connect with our inner selves, fostering self-discovery and inner growth.

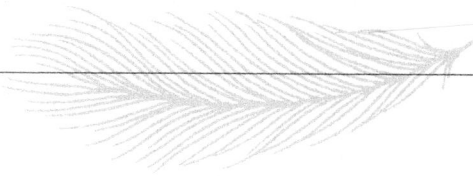

January 28th

"Your words have the power to uplift or wound. Choose them wisely."

- Words carry immense power. By consciously choosing our words and using them to uplift and inspire, we create positive impacts on ourselves and those around us.

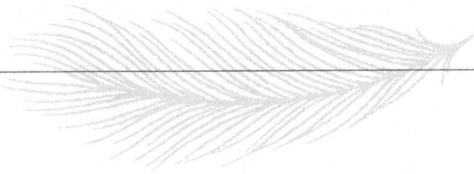

January 29th

"Practice self-compassion, for it is the foundation of emotional well-being."

- Self-compassion involves treating ourselves with kindness and understanding. By practicing self-compassion, we cultivate emotional well-being and foster resilience in the face of challenges.

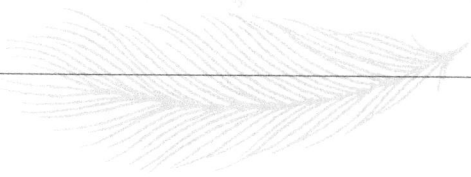

January 30th

"Embrace the unknown, for it holds the magic of infinite possibilities."

- The unknown may feel intimidating, but within it lies immense potential. By embracing the mystery of the unknown, we open ourselves up to magical and transformative experiences.

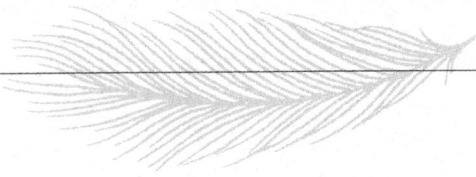

January 31st

"Forgive yourself for past mistakes and allow yourself to grow."

- We all make mistakes, and self-forgiveness is crucial for personal growth. By releasing self-judgment and embracing self-forgiveness, we create space for growth and transformation.

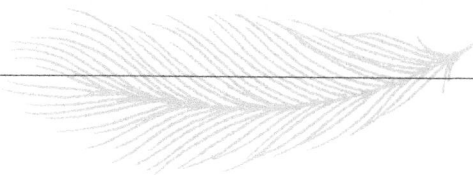

February 1st

"Choose love as your guiding principle in every interaction."

- Love is a powerful force that can transform relationships and interactions. By choosing love as our guiding principle, we foster understanding, compassion, and deep connections with others.

February 2nd

"Celebrate your achievements, no matter how small. Each step forward counts."

- Celebrating achievements, no matter how small, reinforces positive momentum and cultivates a sense of accomplishment. Each step forward is a testament to personal growth.

February 3rd

"Detach from outcomes and surrender to the flow of life."

- Detaching from specific outcomes allows us to surrender to the natural flow of life. By embracing the present moment and releasing attachment, we invite serenity and trust into our lives.

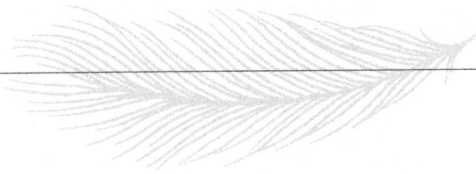

February 4th

"Practice mindfulness, for it anchors you in the beauty of the present moment."

- Mindfulness is the practice of being fully present and engaged in the present moment. By cultivating mindfulness, we heighten our awareness, enhance our experiences, and find inner peace.

February 5th

"Your strength lies in vulnerability. Allow yourself to be seen and heard."

- Vulnerability is a courageous act that allows us to connect deeply with others. By embracing vulnerability, we create spaces for authentic connection and personal growth.

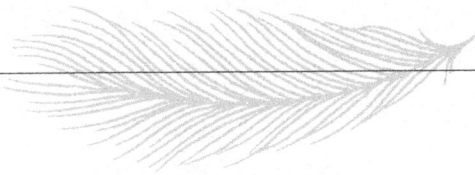

February 6th

"Let go of labels and embrace the vastness of your being."

- Labels limit our potential and confine us to narrow definitions. By letting go of labels and embracing the vastness of our being, we tap into our true essence and live more expansively.

February 7th

"Choose forgiveness over resentment, for it
sets you free."

– Forgiveness liberates the heart and frees us
from the chains of resentment. By choosing
forgiveness, we release ourselves from
emotional burdens and create space for
healing and growth.

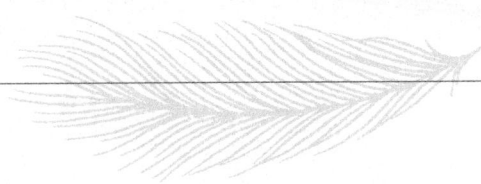

February 8th

"Your intuition is a guiding compass. Trust it."

– Intuition is our inner wisdom, always guiding us toward what serves our highest good. By cultivating trust in our intuition, we align with our authentic selves and make choices that resonate with our souls.

February 9th

"Embrace discomfort as a sign that you are stretching beyond your limits."

- Discomfort often accompanies growth. By embracing discomfort, we recognize it as a sign that we are stretching beyond our limits and moving closer to our full potential.

February 10th

"Focus on progress, not perfection, on your journey of personal growth."

- Perfection is an illusion that can hinder progress. By shifting our focus to progress rather than perfection, we acknowledge that growth is a continuous process and celebrate each step forward.

February 11th

"Embrace simplicity and find beauty in the present moment."

- Simplicity allows us to appreciate the beauty of the present moment. By simplifying our lives, we cultivate a sense of gratitude and deepen our connection with the richness of life's experiences.

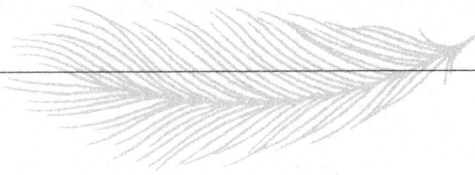

February 12 th

"Practice self-acceptance and embrace all aspects of yourself."

- Self-acceptance involves embracing all aspects of ourselves, including our flaws and imperfections. By loving and accepting ourselves unconditionally, we create a foundation for personal growth and transformation.

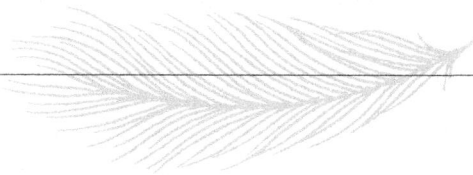

February 13th

"Your energy is a precious resource. Invest it wisely."

– Our energy is finite and needs to be nurtured and protected. By consciously investing our energy in activities, relationships, and pursuits that align with our values, we cultivate a more fulfilling and purposeful life.

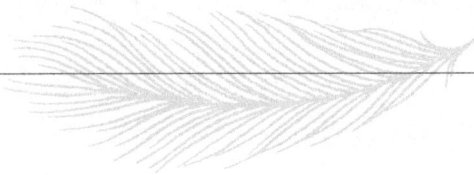

February 14th

"Embrace the power of 'No' to create boundaries and protect your well-being."

- Saying "no" when necessary is an act of self-care and boundary setting. By honouring our own needs and setting healthy boundaries, we protect our well-being and foster personal growth.

February 15th

" Practice self-awareness to uncover your deepest desires and passions."

- Self-awareness is the key to uncovering our deepest desires and passions. By developing a keen understanding of ourselves, we can align our actions with our authentic desires and live a more fulfilling life.

February 16th

"Let go of the need for approval. Your worth is inherent."

- Seeking external approval often leads to a never-ending cycle of validation. By letting go of the need for approval and recognizing our inherent worth, we cultivate a sense of self-validation and empowerment.

February 17th

"Embrace the beauty of impermanence. Change is the only constant."

- Impermanence is a natural part of life. By embracing the beauty of impermanence, we learn to navigate change with grace, adaptability, and an open heart.

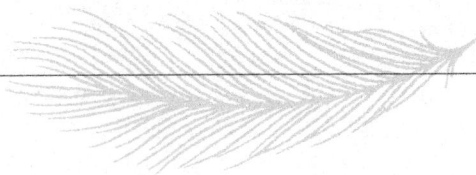

February 18th

"Release attachment to outcomes and find peace in the process."

- Attachment to specific outcomes can lead to disappointment and frustration. By releasing attachment and finding peace in the process, we embrace the journey and open ourselves up to unexpected possibilities.

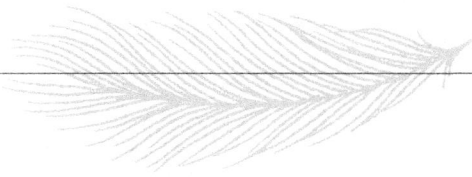

February 19th

"Practice forgiveness, not for others, but for your own healing."

- Forgiveness is not about condoning the actions of others; it is about freeing ourselves from the burden of resentment. By practicing forgiveness, we prioritize our own emotional well-being and invite healing into our lives.

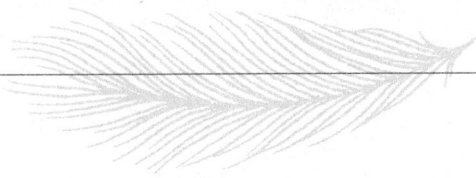

February 20th

"Choose kindness, for it ripples out and creates a more compassionate world."

- Kindness is contagious. By choosing kindness in our interactions with others, we create a ripple effect that spreads compassion and positivity, making the world a better place.

February 21st

"Cultivate resilience and bounce back stronger from life's challenges."

- Resilience is the ability to bounce back from adversity. By cultivating resilience, we develop inner strength, adaptability, and the capacity to overcome obstacles on our path to personal growth.

February 22nd

"Embrace the power of 'I am.' Affirm your inherent worth and potential."

- The words "I am" hold immense power. By affirming our inherent worth, potential, and positive qualities, we shape our self-perception and manifest our desires.

February 23rd

"Practice self-compassion in times of difficulty. You are doing your best."

- Self-compassion involves extending kindness and understanding to ourselves in times of difficulty. By acknowledging that we are doing our best, we cultivate self-support and resilience.

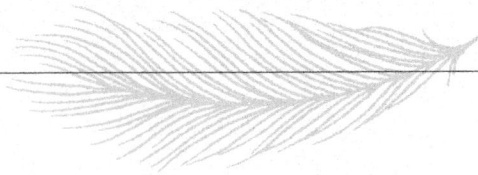

February 24th

"Embrace uncertainty as an invitation to step into the unknown."

- Uncertainty can be intimidating, but it also presents opportunities for growth and self-discovery. By embracing uncertainty as an invitation to step into the unknown, we open ourselves up to new possibilities.

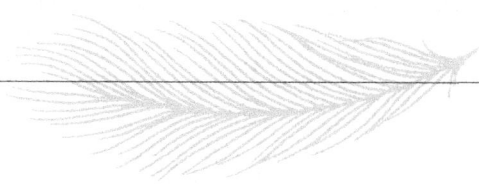

February 25th

"Your worth is not determined by external achievements. You are enough."

- Our worth is not contingent upon external achievements or validation. By recognizing our intrinsic worth, we free ourselves from the need for external validation and cultivate self-acceptance.

February 26th

"Nurture your relationships with love, respect, and open communication."

- Relationships flourish when they are nurtured with love, respect, and open communication. By investing time and energy into cultivating healthy relationships, we create a foundation for personal growth and connection.

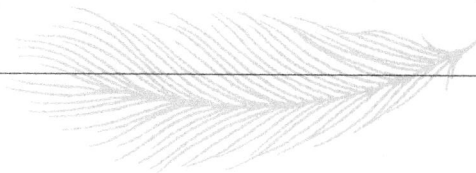

February 27th

"Embrace solitude as an opportunity for self-reflection and self-discovery."

- Solitude allows us to recharge, reflect, and connect with our inner selves. By embracing moments of solitude, we foster self-awareness and uncover insights that fuel personal growth.

February 28th

"Practice empathy and seek to understand the experiences of others."

- Empathy is the ability to put ourselves in someone else's shoes and understand their experiences. By practicing empathy, we foster deeper connections, promote compassion, and cultivate personal growth.

March 1st

"Let go of the need to control. Trust in the unfolding of life."

- The need for control often stems from fear and limits our growth. By letting go of control and trusting in the natural unfolding of life, we surrender to the divine flow and invite serenity into our lives.

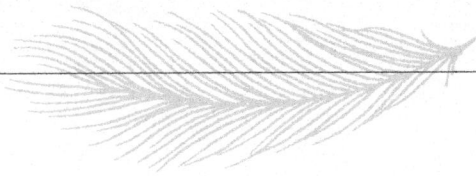

March 2nd

"Embrace self-discipline as a path to personal freedom and growth."

- Self-discipline is the key to achieving our goals and creating positive habits. By embracing self-discipline, we cultivate focus, resilience, and personal freedom.

March 3rd

"Celebrate your uniqueness. You are a masterpiece in progress."

- Each person is a unique masterpiece in progress. By celebrating our uniqueness, we embrace our individuality, appreciate our journey, and honour our own path of personal growth.

March 4th

"Practice active listening and engage fully in your conversations."

- Active listening involves fully engaging in conversations and giving others our undivided attention. By practicing active listening, we foster deeper connections, understanding, and meaningful exchanges.

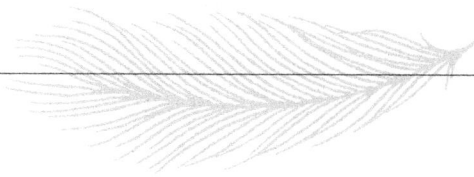

March 5th

"Let go of the need for external validation. Your worth is inherent."

- Seeking external validation traps us in a cycle of dependence. By letting go of the need for external validation and recognizing our inherent worth, we cultivate self-validation and a stronger sense of self.

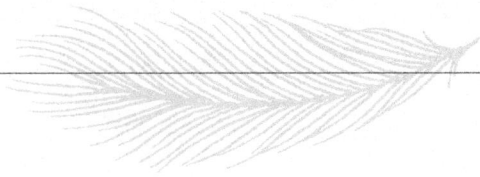

March 6th

" Happiness is not found in possessions but in the gratitude for life's simplest joys."

- True happiness is derived from appreciating the little things and finding contentment in life's everyday pleasures.

March 7th

"Choose compassion over judgment, for everyone is fighting their own battles."

- Compassion allows us to see beyond judgments and recognize that everyone is going through their own challenges. By choosing compassion, we cultivate understanding, empathy, and connection.

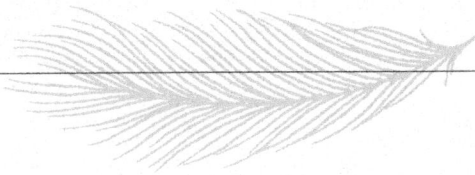

March 8th

"Practice mindfulness in your daily activities and savour the present moment."

- Mindfulness involves being fully present and engaged in our daily activities. By practicing mindfulness, we deepen our experiences, reduce stress, and cultivate a sense of peace and fulfilment.

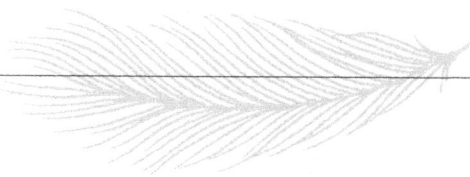

March 9th

"Let go of the past and embrace the infinite possibilities of the present."

- Holding onto the past prevents us from fully embracing the present moment. By letting go of the past and embracing the infinite possibilities of the present, we create space for new experiences and growth.

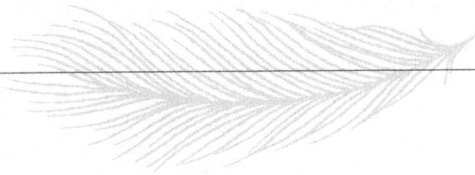

March 10th

"Your voice matters. Speak your truth with courage and conviction."

- Each person has a unique voice and perspective that deserves to be heard. By speaking our truth with courage and conviction, we honour ourselves and contribute to positive change.

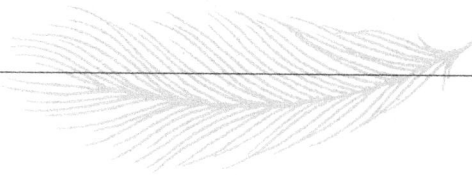

March 11th

"Embrace the lessons within failures. They are stepping stones to success."

- Failures are not setbacks but opportunities for growth and learning. By embracing the lessons within failures, we gain valuable insights and pave the way for future success.

March 12th

"Choose self-care as an act of self-love and nourishment."

- Self-care is an act of self-love that nurtures our mind, body, and soul. By prioritizing self-care, we recharge our energy, cultivate well-being, and show ourselves the love and care we deserve.

March 13th

"Your past does not define your future. You have the power to create a new narrative."

- The past does not dictate our future. By recognizing our power to create a new narrative, we break free from limiting beliefs and embrace the limitless possibilities of personal growth.

March 14th

"Embrace the power of gratitude to transform your perspective."

- Gratitude has the power to shift our perspective and invite abundance into our lives. By cultivating gratitude, we focus on the blessings rather than the challenges, creating a positive outlook on life.

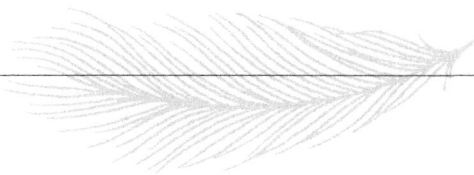

March 15th

"Practice self-empowerment. You hold the key to your own happiness."

- Self-empowerment involves taking ownership of our happiness and well-being. By recognizing our inherent power and taking proactive steps toward personal growth, we create a fulfilling and joyful life.

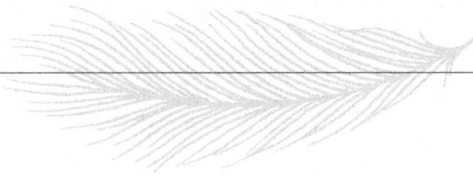

March 16th

"Release the need for external validation. Your opinion of yourself matters most."

- Seeking external validation can be a never-ending pursuit. By releasing the need for external validation and recognizing that our opinion of ourselves matters most, we cultivate self-worth and inner strength.

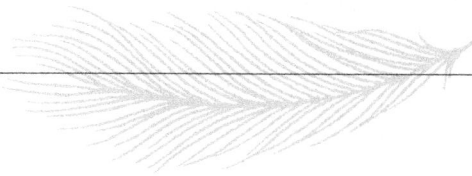

March 17th

"Embrace uncertainty as an invitation to step into your courage."

- Uncertainty often brings fear, but it is also an opportunity to tap into our courage and resilience. By embracing uncertainty as an invitation to step into our courage, we expand our comfort zones and grow as individuals.

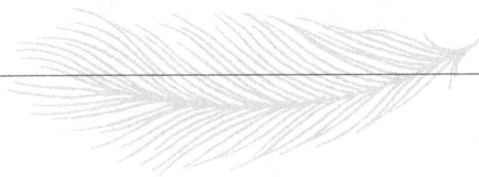

March 18th

"Celebrate the small victories on your journey. They pave the way to big achievements."

- Small victories are significant milestones on our journey of personal growth. By celebrating these moments, we acknowledge our progress, boost our confidence, and pave the way for even greater achievements.

March 19th

"Choose love and compassion in the face of anger or negativity."

- Love and compassion are powerful antidotes to anger and negativity. By choosing love and compassion, we cultivate understanding, promote harmony, and contribute to a more peaceful world.

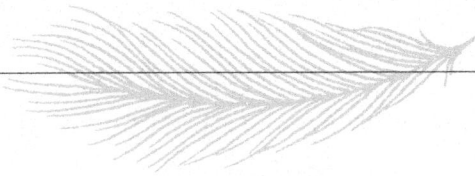

March 20th

"Nurture your creativity and unleash the magic within."

- Creativity is a wellspring of inspiration and self-expression. By nurturing our creativity, we tap into our innate potential, unlock new possibilities, and infuse our lives with magic.

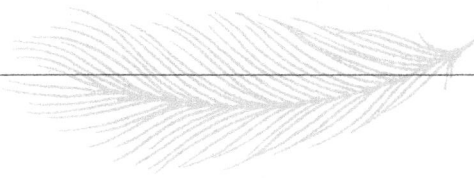

March 21st

"Practice forgiveness, not to forget, but to set yourself free."

- Forgiveness is not about forgetting the past but freeing ourselves from its emotional burden. By practicing forgiveness, we release negative attachments, foster healing, and create space for personal growth.

March 22nd

"Embrace the journey of self-discovery. You are an ever-evolving masterpiece."

- Self-discovery is a lifelong journey. By embracing this journey with curiosity and openness, we uncover layers of our authentic selves and realize that we are ever-evolving masterpieces.

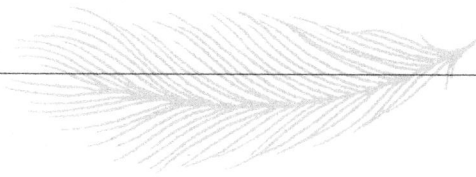

March 23rd

"Choose patience in times of uncertainty. Your path will unfold in due time."

- Patience is a virtue that allows us to navigate uncertainty with grace and trust. By choosing patience, we surrender to the natural unfolding of our path, knowing that everything will come together in due time.

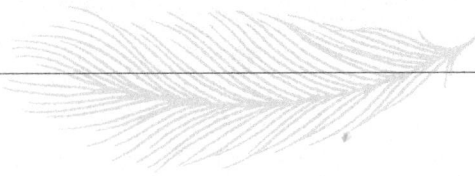

March 24th

"Find joy in the present moment, for it is where life truly happens."

- Joy resides in the present moment. By fully embracing and savouring each moment, we tap into the richness of life's experiences and cultivate a deeper sense of contentment and fulfilment.

March 25th

"Practice gratitude for the lessons within challenges. They shape your growth."

- Challenges hold valuable lessons that shape our growth. By practicing gratitude for these lessons, we shift our perspective from victimhood to empowerment and embrace the transformative power of adversity.

March 26th

"Let go of the need to be right. Embrace the beauty of diverse perspectives."

- The need to be right often creates conflicts and hinders personal growth. By letting go of this need and embracing diverse perspectives, we foster understanding, empathy, and personal expansion.

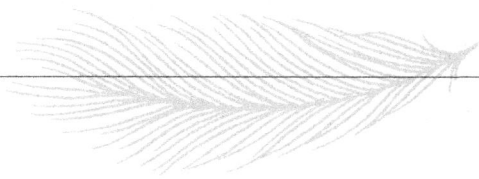

March 27th

"Embrace the power of 'Yes.' Say yes to new experiences and opportunities."

- Saying yes to new experiences and opportunities opens doors to personal growth and self-discovery. By embracing the power of "yes," we expand our horizons and invite transformative experiences into our lives.

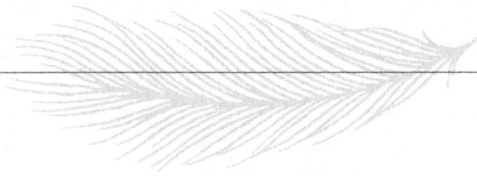

March 28th

"Choose self-compassion in times of self-doubt. You are deserving of love and understanding."

- Self-compassion is a balm for self-doubt. By choosing self-compassion, we counter self-criticism with self-love and understanding, fostering self-acceptance and resilience.

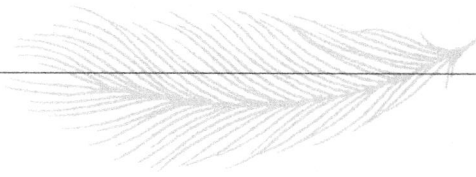

March 29th

"Find inspiration in the beauty of nature. It holds wisdom and healing."

- Nature is a wellspring of inspiration, wisdom, and healing. By immersing ourselves in the beauty of nature, we connect with its serenity and tap into its transformative power.

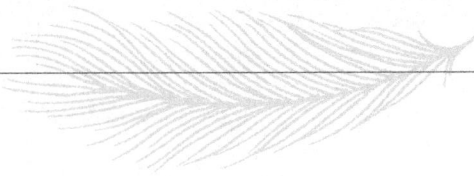

March 30th

"Embrace the art of letting go. Release what no longer serves you."

- Letting go is a powerful act of liberation and personal growth. By releasing what no longer serves us, we create space for new opportunities, experiences, and relationships that align with our authentic selves.

March 31st

"Practice self-reflection as a mirror to your inner world."

- Self-reflection is a mirror that reveals the depths of our inner world. By practicing self-reflection, we gain self-awareness, uncover insights, and nurture personal growth.

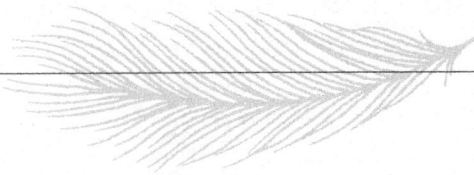

April 1st

"Choose forgiveness, not for others, but for your own peace of mind."

- Forgiveness is an act of liberation that brings peace of mind. By choosing forgiveness, we release ourselves from the shackles of resentment and create space for inner peace and healing.

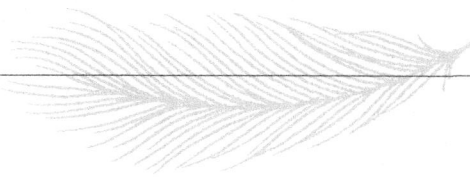

April 2nd

"Embrace authenticity and let your true self shine."

- Authenticity is a beautiful expression of our true selves. By embracing authenticity, we honour our uniqueness, live with integrity, and inspire others to do the same.

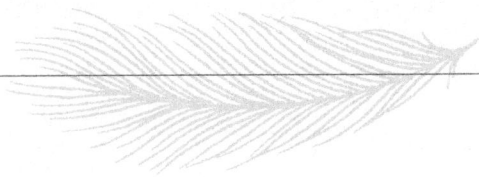

April 3rd

"Celebrate the journey, not just the destination. Each step is part of your growth."

- The journey is as important as the destination. By celebrating each step along the way, we acknowledge our growth, find joy in the process, and create a meaningful and fulfilling life.

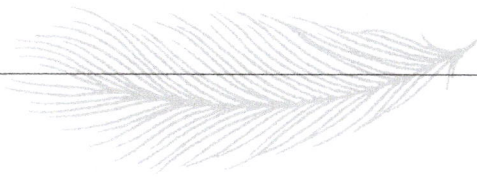

April 4th

"Choose self-care as an act of self-love and rejuvenation."

- Self-care is an act of self-love and rejuvenation. By prioritizing self-care, we honour our well-being, replenish our energy, and show ourselves the love and care we deserve.

April 5th

"Embrace the power of positive affirmations. They shape your reality."

- Positive affirmations are powerful tools for shaping our reality. By consciously choosing positive thoughts and affirmations, we shift our mindset, cultivate self-belief, and attract positive experiences.

April 6th

"Release the need for external validation. You are enough as you are."

- External validation is temporary and unreliable. By releasing the need for external validation and recognizing our inherent worth, we embrace self-acceptance and live authentically as our true selves.

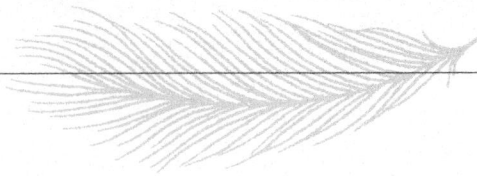

April 7th

"Practice gratitude for the abundance that surrounds you."

- Gratitude opens the door to abundance. By practicing gratitude for the blessings and abundance in our lives, we attract more positive experiences and cultivate a sense of fulfilment and contentment.

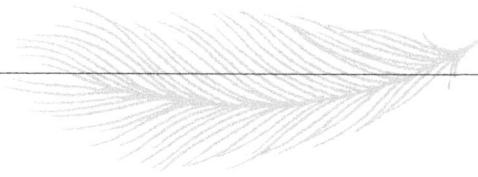

April 8th

"Embrace change as an opportunity for growth and self-transformation."

- Change can be intimidating, but it also holds immense potential for growth and self-transformation. By embracing change with an open mind and heart, we adapt, evolve, and discover new aspects of ourselves.

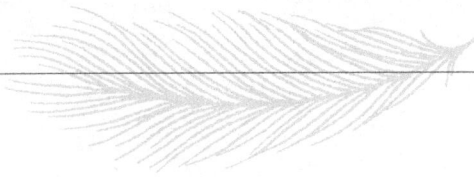

April 9th

"Choose self-empowerment over victimhood. You have the power to shape your destiny."

- Self-empowerment is a conscious choice to take ownership of our lives. By choosing self-empowerment over victimhood, we tap into our innate power, shape our destiny, and create the life we desire.

April 10th

"Embrace the beauty of simplicity. It paves the way for clarity and peace."

- Simplicity brings clarity and peace. By embracing simplicity in our thoughts, actions, and surroundings, we create space for inner stillness, clarity, and a deeper connection with ourselves.

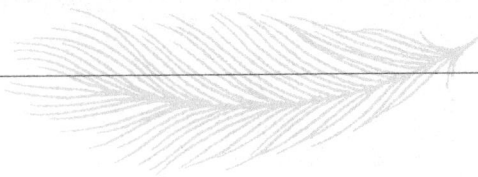

April 11th

"Let go of attachments and embrace the freedom of detachment."

- Attachments can create suffering and limit our growth. By letting go of attachments and embracing detachment, we cultivate freedom, flow, and a greater sense of inner peace.

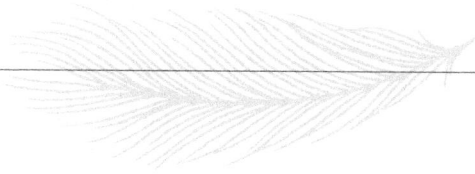

April 12th

"Practice mindfulness in your daily interactions. Be fully present."

- Mindfulness is the art of being fully present and engaged in the present moment. By practicing mindfulness in our daily interactions, we deepen our connections, communicate effectively, and foster deeper understanding.

April 13th

"Release the need to compare yourself to others. Your journey is unique."

- Comparison robs us of joy and hinders personal growth. By releasing the need to compare ourselves to others and embracing the uniqueness of our own journey, we cultivate self-acceptance and focus on our own progress.

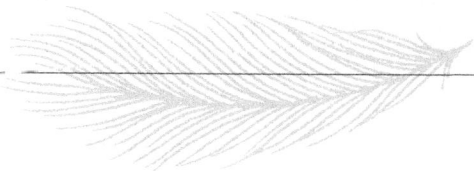

April 14th

"Embrace challenges as opportunities for growth and self-discovery."

- Challenges provide fertile ground for growth and self-discovery. By embracing challenges with courage and resilience, we unlock our full potential, gain valuable insights, and evolve as individuals.

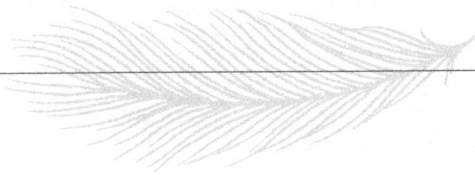

April 15th

"The sky is vast, and so are your dreams. So, dream big and fearlessly soar."

- Think beyond limits and dream ambitiously. Just as the sky has no boundaries, neither should aspiration.

April 16th

"Embrace the power of vulnerability. It cultivates deeper connections."

- Vulnerability is the gateway to authentic connections. By embracing vulnerability and showing up as our true selves, we foster deeper connections, trust, and intimacy in our relationships.

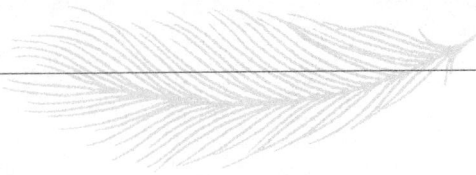

April 17th

"Celebrate the small victories on your journey. They pave the way to bigger achievements."

- Celebrating small victories along the way fuels our motivation and self-belief. By acknowledging and celebrating each small victory, we build momentum and create a foundation for bigger achievements.

April 18th

"Choose gratitude as a daily practice. It transforms your perspective."

- Gratitude is a transformative practice. By choosing gratitude as a daily habit, we shift our perspective from scarcity to abundance, cultivating joy, and attracting more blessings into our lives.

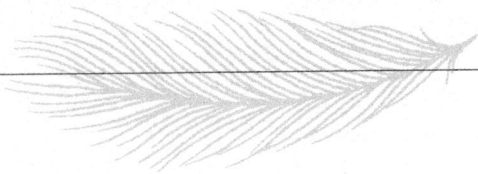

April 19th

"Embrace solitude as an opportunity for self-reflection and inner growth."

- Solitude provides a sacred space for self-reflection and inner growth. By embracing moments of solitude, we nourish our souls, deepen our self-awareness, and foster personal transformation.

April 20th

" Practice active listening to honour others' experiences and foster understanding."

- Active listening involves giving our full attention and presence to others. By practicing active listening, we honour others' experiences, foster empathy, and create deeper connections.

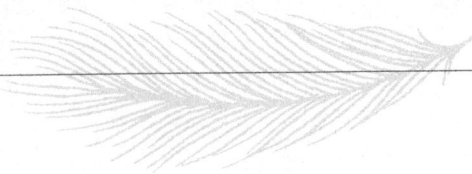

April 21st

"Let go of the need for perfection. Embrace the beauty of imperfection."

- Perfectionism is an illusion that hinders personal growth. By letting go of the need for perfection and embracing the beauty of imperfection, we allow ourselves to be authentic, vulnerable, and fully human.

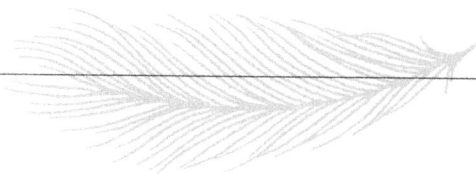

April 22nd

"Choose self-acceptance and embrace all aspects of yourself."

- Self-acceptance involves embracing all aspects of ourselves, including our flaws and imperfections. By practicing self-acceptance, we cultivate self-love, inner peace, and a strong foundation for personal growth.

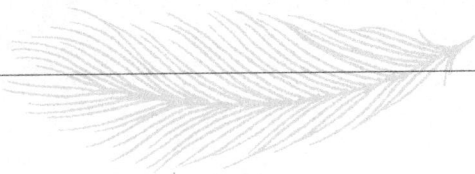

April 23rd

"Success is not a destination but a journey of self-discovery and growth."

- Success is not merely reaching a specific point; it is an ongoing process of learning, evolving, and becoming the best version of ourselves.

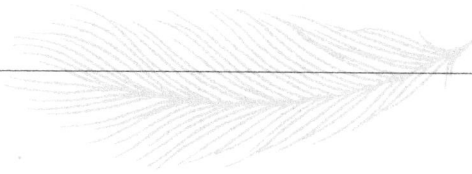

April 24th

"Choose self-care as a sacred act of self-love and nourishment."

- Self-care is a sacred act of self-love and nourishment. By prioritizing self-care, we honour our well-being, replenish our energy, and create a solid foundation for personal growth.

April 25th

"Embrace change as a catalyst for growth and transformation."

- Change is a constant in life. By embracing change as a catalyst for growth and transformation, we adapt, evolve, and open ourselves up to new possibilities and experiences.

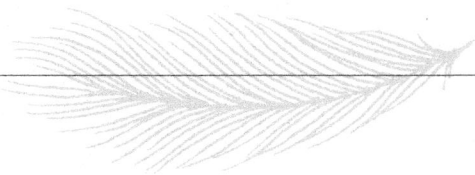

April 26th

"The only way to discover your limits is to push past them with relentless determination"

- True growth and self-discovery come from challenging ourselves and embracing the discomfort that accompanies it.

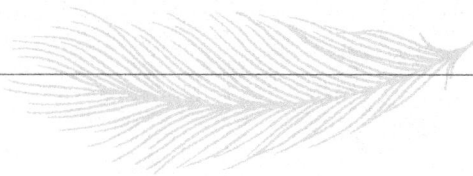

April 27th

"Embrace the power of vulnerability. It opens doors to authenticity and growth."

- Vulnerability is the gateway to authenticity and personal growth. By embracing vulnerability, we open ourselves up to deeper connections, self-discovery, and meaningful experiences.

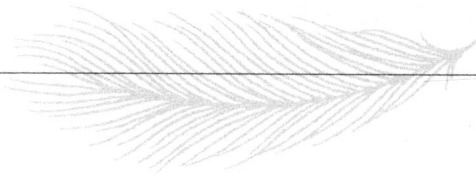

April 28th

"Celebrate your uniqueness. It is your superpower."

- Each person is unique and possesses their own set of strengths and gifts. By celebrating our uniqueness, we embrace our individuality, live authentically, and tap into our true power.

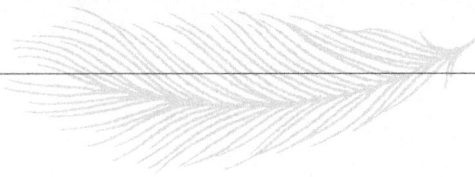

April 29th

"Choose forgiveness as a path to liberation and inner peace."

- Forgiveness is a path to liberation and inner peace. By choosing forgiveness, we release ourselves from the chains of resentment and find freedom in our hearts and minds.

April 30th

"Embrace the beauty of simplicity. It brings clarity and peace to your life."

- Simplicity brings clarity and peace to our lives. By embracing simplicity, we let go of excess, declutter our minds and spaces, and create room for what truly matters.

May 1st

"Surrender to the flow of life, and it will carry you to unexpected places."

- Trust in the natural flow of life, and it will lead you to new opportunities and unforeseen destinations.

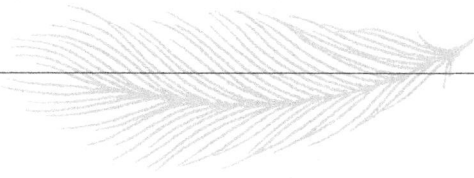

May 2nd

"Practice mindfulness in your daily routines. Be fully present in each moment."

- Mindfulness is the practice of being fully present and engaged in each moment. By practicing mindfulness in our daily routines, we cultivate awareness, reduce stress, and enhance our overall well-being.

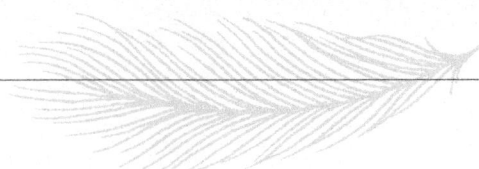

May 3rd

"Let go of the need for external validation. Your worth comes from within."

- Seeking external validation can be a never-ending cycle. By letting go of the need for external validation, we recognize that our worth comes from within, fostering self-acceptance and self-empowerment.

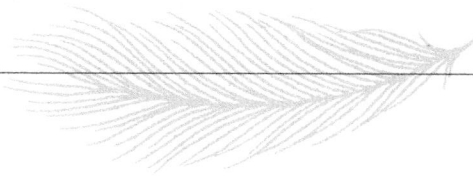

May 4th

"Embrace uncertainty as an opportunity for growth and self-discovery."

- Uncertainty may be uncomfortable, but it is also an opportunity for growth and self-discovery. By embracing uncertainty with an open mind, we develop resilience, expand our comfort zones, and uncover new possibilities.

May 5th

"Choose self-empowerment over self-doubt. You have the power to create your reality."

- Self-empowerment is choosing to believe in our abilities and taking control of our lives. By choosing self-empowerment over self-doubt, we unlock our potential, take action, and shape our own reality.

May 6th

"Embrace the journey, not just the destination. Every step is a part of your growth."

- The journey is as important as the destination. By embracing the journey, we appreciate the growth, lessons, and experiences along the way, making the destination more meaningful.

May 7th

"Practice gratitude for the simple pleasures in life. They bring joy and fulfilment."

- Gratitude for the simple pleasures in life cultivates joy and fulfilment. By practicing gratitude for the little things, we shift our focus to the blessings that surround us and find happiness in the present moment.

May 8th

"Embrace the power of positive self-talk. Your words shape your reality."

- Positive self-talk has the power to shape our reality. By choosing uplifting and empowering words, we cultivate a positive mindset, boost our self-confidence, and attract positive experiences.

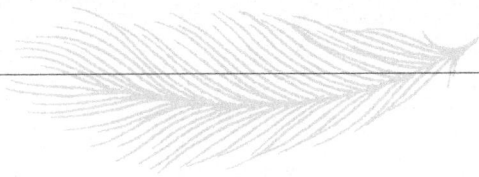

May 9th

"Release attachments and trust in the flow of life. Everything unfolds as it should."

- Releasing attachments allows us to trust in the flow of life. By surrendering to the natural unfolding, we let go of resistance, find peace, and allow things to fall into place in divine timing.

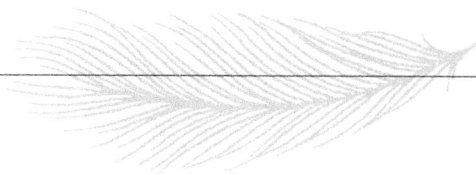

May 10th

"Choose self-compassion in times of struggle. Treat yourself with kindness and understanding."

- Self-compassion is essential during times of struggle. By treating ourselves with kindness and understanding, we provide the support and nurturing we need to navigate challenges with grace and resilience.

May 11th

"Embrace the power of self-reflection. It reveals insights and fosters growth."

- Self-reflection is a powerful practice that uncovers insights and fosters personal growth. By taking time to reflect on our thoughts, actions, and experiences, we gain self-awareness and move forward with intention and clarity.

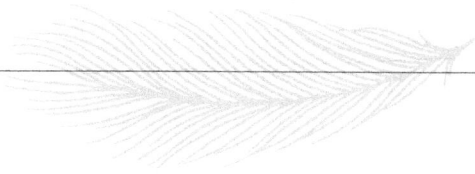

May 12th

"Celebrate your progress, no matter how small. Each step counts."

- Celebrating progress, no matter how small, is essential for motivation and self-belief. By acknowledging and celebrating each step forward, we reinforce positive momentum and fuel our continued growth.

May 13th

"Choose authenticity over conformity. You are meant to shine as your unique self."

- Authenticity is choosing to be true to ourselves rather than conforming to societal expectations. By choosing authenticity, we honour our uniqueness, express our truth, and inspire others to do the same.

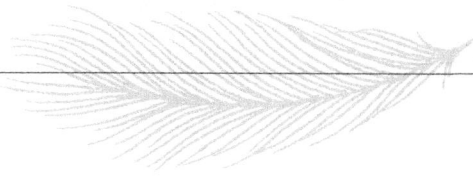

May 14th

"Practice self-care as a priority. Nurture your well-being in mind, body, and spirit."

- Self-care is a priority for nurturing our overall well-being. By prioritizing self-care in mind, body, and spirit, we replenish our energy, reduce stress, and cultivate a healthy and balanced life.

May 15th

"Embrace the lessons within failures. They are opportunities for growth and learning."

- Failures provide valuable lessons for growth and learning. By embracing these lessons, we gain wisdom, resilience, and the courage to persevere on our path to success.

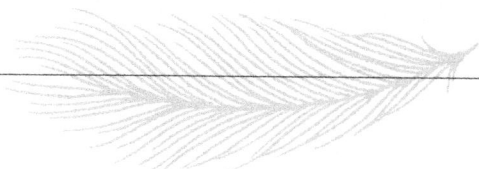

May 16th

"Choose self-acceptance over self-judgment. You are worthy of love and belonging."

- Self-acceptance is choosing to love and accept ourselves unconditionally. By embracing self-acceptance, we let go of self-judgment, cultivate self-worth, and foster deep inner peace.

May 17th

"Embrace the power of silence. It holds clarity and wisdom."

- Silence is a powerful teacher that holds clarity and wisdom. By embracing moments of silence, we quiet the noise around us and connect with our inner wisdom, finding answers and peace within.

May 18th

"Embrace your uniqueness, for in your individuality lies your true power."

- Celebrate our distinct qualities and talents, as they are what make us stand out and bring value to the world.

May 19th

"The greatest act of kindness is to be compassionate to yourself."

- Self-compassion is the foundation or extending genuine kindness and understanding to others.

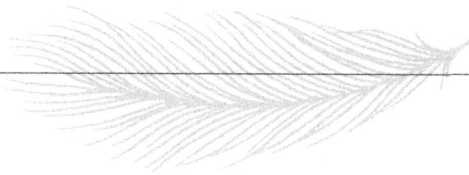

May 20th

"Embrace solitude as an opportunity for self-discovery and inner peace."

- Solitude provides a sanctuary for self-discovery and inner peace. By embracing moments of solitude, we connect with our true selves, gain clarity, and nurture our spiritual growth.

May 21st

"Practice active listening to honour others' experiences and foster deeper connections."

- Active listening is a gift we can offer to others. By practicing active listening, we create space for understanding, empathy, and deeper connections, fostering harmonious relationships and personal growth.

May 22nd

"Let go of the need for perfection. Embrace the beauty of your imperfections."

- Perfection is an illusion that stifles growth. By letting go of the need for perfection and embracing the beauty of our imperfections, we celebrate our uniqueness and open ourselves to self-acceptance and personal growth.

May 23rd

"Choose self-compassion in times of self-doubt. Treat yourself with kindness and understanding."

- Self-compassion is a gentle response to self-doubt. By treating ourselves with kindness and understanding, we nurture our inner selves, build resilience, and cultivate a loving relationship with ourselves.

May 24th

"Embrace the power of vulnerability. It fosters authentic connections and growth."

- Vulnerability is the gateway to authentic connections and personal growth. By embracing vulnerability, we allow ourselves to be seen and heard, fostering deeper relationships, and expanding our capacity for love and joy.

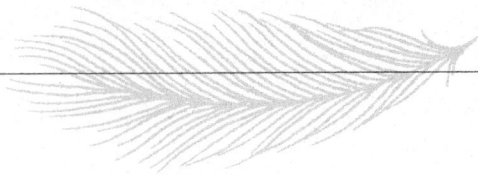

May 25th

"Celebrate the small steps on your journey. They lead to significant transformation."

- Celebrating the small steps on our journey is vital. Each step, no matter how small, contributes to significant transformation and progress. By acknowledging and honouring these steps, we find inspiration and momentum to continue growing.

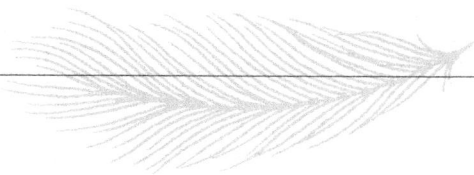

May 26th

"Choose gratitude for the lessons within challenges. They shape your strength and resilience."

- Challenges hold valuable lessons that shape our strength and resilience. By practicing gratitude for these lessons, we shift our perspective, find silver linings, and cultivate the inner fortitude to overcome obstacles.

May 27th

"Embrace change as an opportunity for growth and adaptation."

- Change is inevitable and offers opportunities for growth and adaptation. By embracing change with an open mind and heart, we learn to navigate transitions, expand our horizons, and embrace new beginnings.

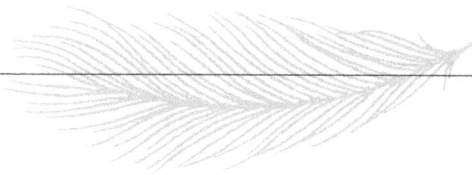

May 28th

"Choose self-empowerment over self-doubt. You have the power to shape your destiny."

- Self-empowerment is choosing to believe in our abilities and take charge of our lives. By choosing self-empowerment over self-doubt, we tap into our innate potential, manifest our desires, and create our own destiny.

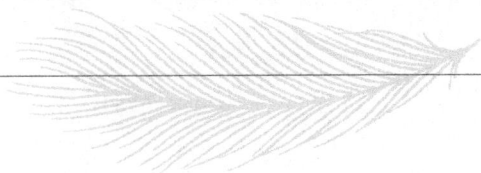

May 29th

"Embrace the journey, not just the destination. Every experience has value."

- The journey itself is valuable, not just the destination. By embracing the journey, we appreciate the growth, lessons, and experiences it offers, making the destination even more meaningful and fulfilling.

May 30th

"Practice gratitude for the simple pleasures in life. They bring joy and contentment."

- Gratitude for the simple pleasures in life amplifies our joy and contentment. By practicing gratitude for the little things, we shift our focus to the blessings around us, foster a positive mindset, and invite more abundance into our lives.

May 31st

"Success is the sum of small efforts done
consistently."

- Consistency in our efforts, no matter how
small, accumulates into significant
achievements.

June 1st

"Your passion is the compass that leads you to your purpose."

- Follow your passions, as they guide you towards a life of purpose and fulfilment.

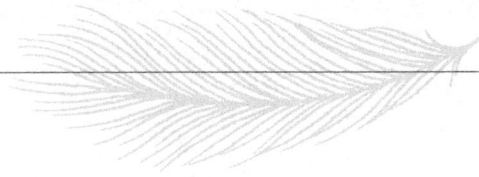

June 2nd

"Your vision becomes clearer when you look inward with an open heart."

- Self-reflection and introspection help us gain clarity about our desires and purpose.

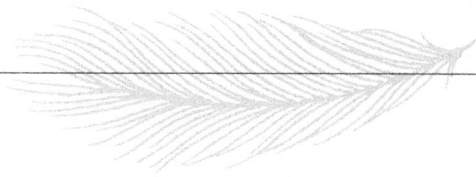

June 3rd

"The magic of life lies in the serenity of the present moment."

- Embrace the present moment to experience the enchanting beauty of life

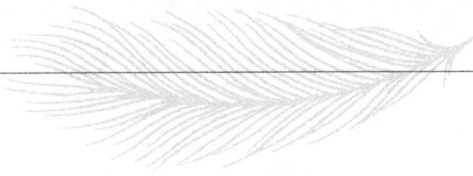

June 4th

"Celebrate your progress, no matter how small. Each step is a victory."

- Celebrating progress, no matter how small, fuels our motivation and self-belief. By acknowledging and celebrating each step forward, we reinforce positive momentum and inspire continued growth.

June 5th

"Choose authenticity over conformity. You are meant to shine as your true self."

- Authenticity is choosing to be true to ourselves rather than conforming to societal expectations. By choosing authenticity, we honour our unique gifts, live in alignment with our values, and inspire others to do the same.

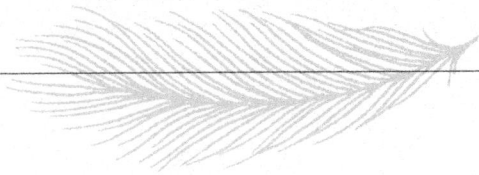

June 6th

"When faced with storms, be the lighthouse that guides others to safety."

-In challenging times, being a source of strength and support for others can make a profound difference. Shine your light even during the darkest moment, helping others find their way through the storms of life.

June 7th

"Dare to be different, for true beauty lies in embracing your uniqueness."

- Embracing out individuality and celebrating what makes us different is a testament to our authenticity. Shine bright and be true to yourself.

June 8th

"Believe in the beauty of your uniqueness,
for it is the gift you bring to the world."

- Embrace your individuality, as it is what
makes you shine brightly and contribute
uniquely to the world.

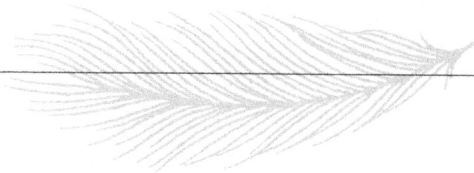

June 9th

"Embrace the power of silence. It holds clarity and serenity."

- Silence is a source of clarity and serenity. By embracing moments of silence, we quiet the noise around us, connect with our inner wisdom, and find answers and peace within.

June 10th

"Celebrate the beauty of the present moment. It is a precious gift."

- The present moment is a precious gift. By celebrating the beauty of the present, we fully engage with life, savour the small joys, and create memories that will be cherished in the future.

June 11th

"Success is not a destination but a journey of self-discovery."

- Success is not a fixes point but a continuous exploration of your capabilities.

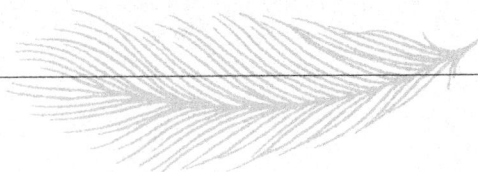

June 12th

"Every ending paves the way for a new and magnificent beginning."

- Embrace the cycles of life, for every ending brings the promise of fresh opportunities.

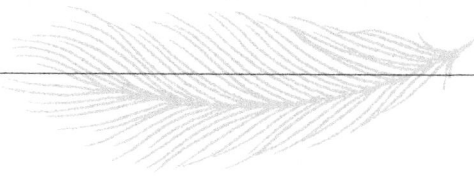

June 13th

"The universe conspires in your favour when you pursue your passions with determination."

- When you passionately pursue your goals, the universe aligns to support your journey.

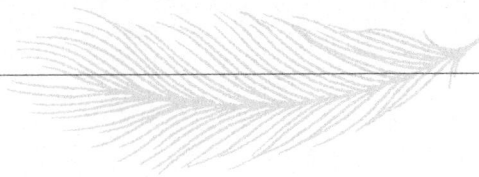

June 14th

"Let go of the need for perfection. Embrace the beauty of your journey."

- Perfection is an illusion that hinders personal growth. By letting go of the need for perfection and embracing the beauty of our journey, we celebrate progress, learn from mistakes, and embrace the joy of continuous growth.

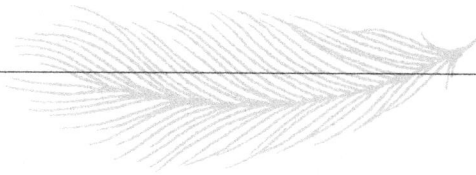

June 15th

"The canvas of your life is coloured by the choices you make."

- Our choices shape the direction and outcome of our lives.

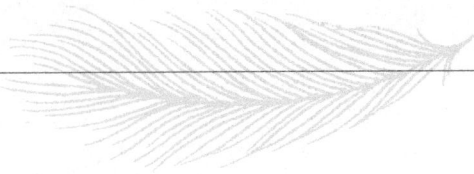

June 16th

"Embrace the power of vulnerability. It strengthens your connections and authenticity."

- Vulnerability is the key to deep connections and authenticity. By embracing vulnerability, we allow ourselves to be seen, heard, and understood, fostering meaningful relationships and personal growth.

June 17th

"Failure is not the end; it's a stepping stone towards success."

- Embracing failure as a learning experience empowers us to persevere and grow stronger on our journey to achieving our goals.

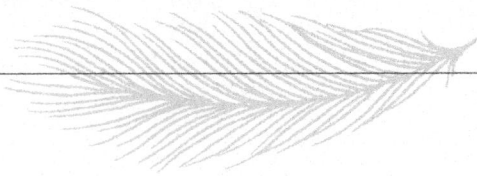

June 18th

"Choose gratitude for the lessons within challenges. They shape your resilience and growth."

- Challenges hold valuable lessons that shape our resilience and growth. By practicing gratitude for these lessons, we shift our perspective, find strength within, and cultivate a positive mindset to overcome obstacles.

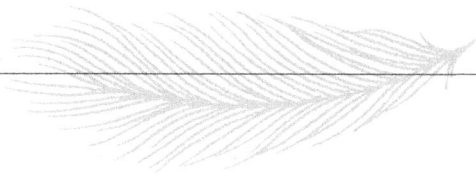

June 19th

"Embrace change as an opportunity for growth and transformation."

- Change is a constant in life, and it provides opportunities for growth and transformation. By embracing change with an open mind and heart, we adapt, evolve, and unlock our full potential.

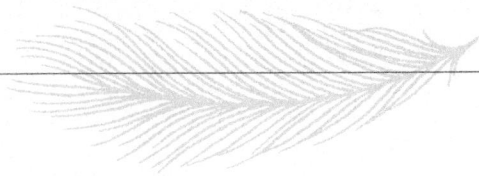

June 20th

"Success is a reflection of your determination to turn dreams into reality."

- Determination and hard work are the driving forces behind achieving success.

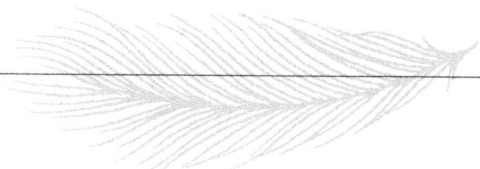

June 21st

"Embrace the journey, not just the destination. Every step holds value."

- The journey itself is meaningful and holds valuable experiences. By embracing the journey, we appreciate the growth, wisdom, and joy it brings, making the destination more fulfilling.

June 22nd

"Practice gratitude for the simple pleasures in life. They bring abundant joy."

- Gratitude for the simple pleasures amplifies our joy. By practicing gratitude for the little things, we shift our focus to the blessings that surround us, cultivate happiness, and invite more abundance into our lives.

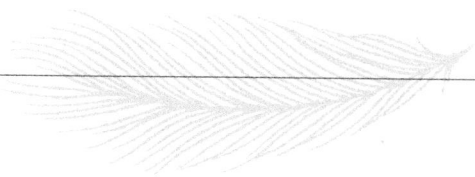

June 23rd

"Embrace change like the seasons; it brings transformation and growth."

- Just as seasons change, so do we. Embrace change as an opportunity for personal evolution.

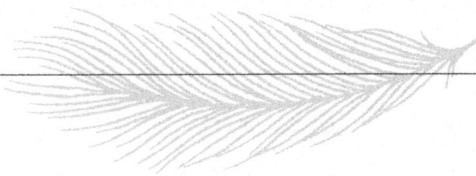

June 24th

"Release attachments and trust in the flow of life. The universe has a plan for you."

- Releasing attachments allows us to trust in the natural flow of life. By surrendering to the universe's plan, we let go of resistance, find inner peace, and open ourselves up to new possibilities and synchronicities.

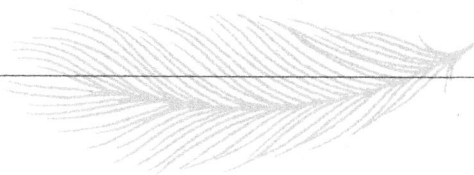

June 25th

"When you let go of the past, you create space for a brighter future."

- Releasing the burdens of the past allows us to move forward with hope and optimism.

June 26th

"Embrace the power of self-reflection. It reveals insights and fosters personal growth."

- Self-reflection is a powerful tool for self-discovery and personal growth. By taking time to reflect on our thoughts, actions, and experiences, we gain self-awareness, clarity, and the wisdom to move forward with intention.

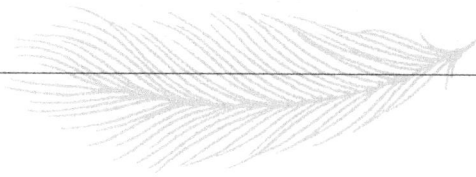

June 27th

"Celebrate your progress, no matter how small. Each step is a testament to your growth."

- Celebrating progress, no matter how small, is essential. Each step forward is a testament to our growth and determination. By acknowledging and celebrating these milestones, we foster motivation and inspire continued progress.

June 28th

"In the pursuit of greatness, remember that every setback is an opportunity for a remarkable comeback."

-See setbacks as stepping stones rather than obstacles. When we embrace resilience and use failures as valuable lessons, we can rise stringer and wiser to achieve greatness.

June 29th

"Life's greatest adventures are often found in moments of spontaneity and daring."

-Taking risks and embracing spontaneity can lead to some of the most memorable experiences. Step outside of your comfort zone and seize the opportunities that come your way.

June 30th

"Turn adversity into strength, for diamonds are forged under pressure."

- Adversity can be transformative, into stronger, more resilient individuals . Like diamonds formed under pressure, we can emerge from difficult times shining brightly.

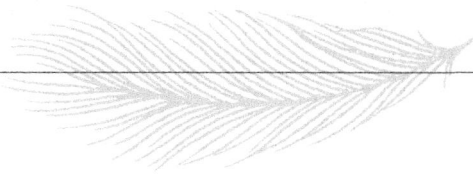

July 1st

"Your thoughts are seeds; plant positivity and watch your life blossom."

- Cultivate a positive mindset, and you'll witness the transformational impact on your experiences.

July 2nd

"Embrace the power of silence. It holds clarity, inspiration, and inner peace."

- Silence is a source of clarity, inspiration, and inner peace. By embracing moments of silence, we quiet the external noise, connect with our inner wisdom, and find answers and tranquillity within.

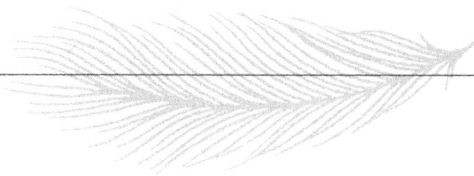

July 3rd

"Your thoughts shape your reality; choose them wisely."

- Our thoughts influence our perceptions and experiences, so focus on cultivating positive ones.

July 4th

"Fear is a compass; let it guide you toward your courage."

- Acknowledge fear, but use it as a guide toward taking brave and bold actions in pursuit of your aspirations.

July 5th

"Be patient with yourself; growth takes time and nurturing."

- Just as plants need time to grow, so do we. Be kind to yourself on your journey of personal development.

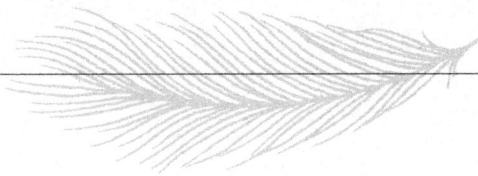

July 6th

"In the darkness of doubt, faith becomes the guiding light."

- Have faith in yourself and your abilities, even during uncertain times.

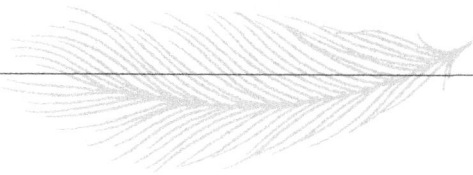

July 7th

"Within the garden of dreams, action is the water that nourishes growth."

- Taking action is essential in realizing the full potential of our dreams.

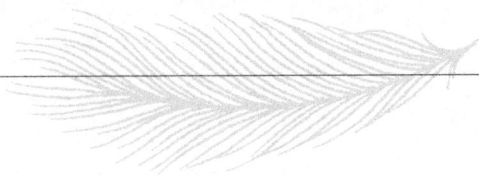

July 8th

"Dare to be audacious; great achievements are born from boldness."

- Extraordinary accomplishments require daring to take bold and courageous actions.

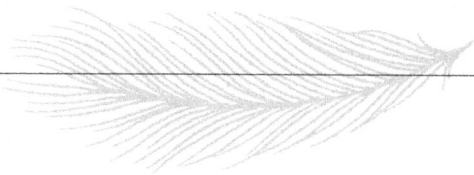

July 9th

"Your uniqueness is the key that unlocks the doors of opportunity."

- Embrace your uniqueness, as it brings forth endless possibilities.

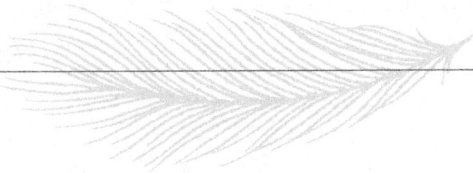

July 10th

"Celebrate the small victories on your journey. They pave the way to significant achievements."

- Celebrating small victories is essential for motivation and self-belief. Each small step forward is a victory on our journey, leading us closer to significant achievements and personal transformation.

July 11th

"Forgiveness is not a weakness; it is an act of strength and liberation."

- Letting go of grudges and embracing forgiveness empowers us to move forward with a lighter heart and a more profound sense of peace

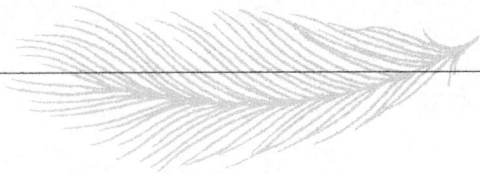

July 12th

"Your dreams are like seeds; nurture them with dedication, and they will bloom."

- Like plants need care and attention to grow, our dreams require dedication and effort to manifest into reality.

July 13th

"Each sunrise brings new hope and the promise of fresh beginnings."

- Each day is an opportunity to start a new and create a brighter future.

July 14th

"Dance with the rhythm of life, and you'll find harmony in every step."

- Embracing life's ups and downs, just as one dances to the beat of music, allows us to find balance and contentment.

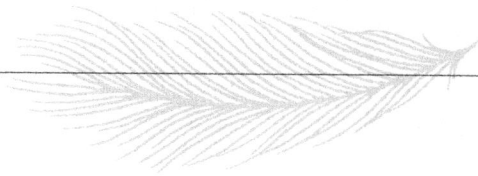

July 15th

"Celebrate your progress, no matter how small, as it inches you closer to your dreams."

- Acknowledging our achievements, no matter how minor, encourages continued effort and motivates us to reach for more significant milestones.

July 16th

"Happiness blooms where gratitude is planted."

- Gratitude nurtures a positive mindset, leading to a more joyful and fulfilling life.

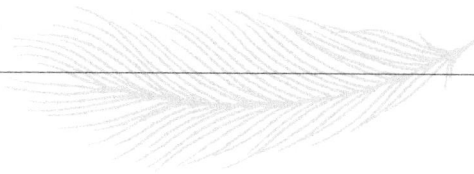

July 17th

"The power of gratitude transforms the ordinary into the extraordinary."

- Gratitude magnifies the joy and significance of even the simplest moments.

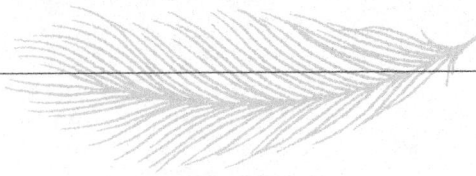

July 18th

"Sow seeds of kindness, and you'll harvest a garden of love."

- Acts of kindness and love have a boomerang effect, returning to enrich our lives.

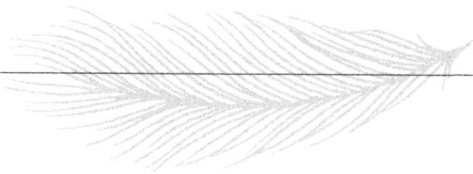

July 19th

"The power of a single act of kindness can light up the world."

- One small act of kindness can have a profound impact on the lives of others.

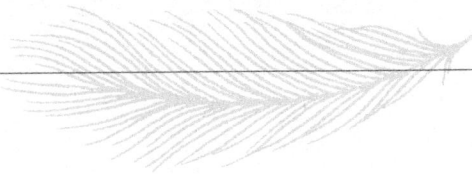

July 20th

"The essence of success is in finding joy in the pursuit of greatness."

- Enjoy the journey towards success, for that is where the true fulfilment lies.

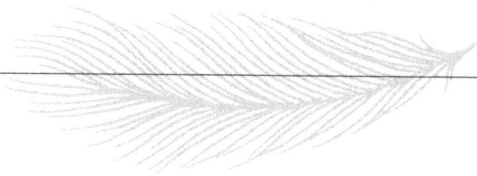

July 21st

"Embrace change, for it is the only constant on the path to progress."

- Change can be intimidating, but it is an essential part of growth and improvement. This quote urges you to welcome change and adapt, as it is the key to moving forward and achieving your goals.

July 22nd

"In the pursuit of knowledge, we discover the boundless wonders of the universe and ourselves."

- Learning is a lifelong journey that not only expands our understanding of the world but also uncovers the depths of our own potential. Celebrate the transformative power of knowledge.

July 23rd

"Live in the present, for it is the only moment where life truly exists."

- The past is gone, and the future is uncertain. The only moment we have control over is the present. Remember to savour the now and make the most of each moment.

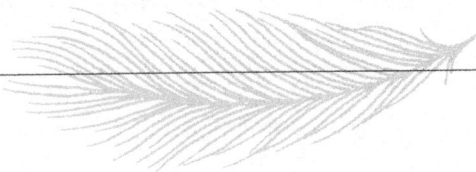

July 24th

"In the garden of life, kindness blooms as the most precious flower."

- Kindness has the power to bring beauty and harmony to our lives and the lives of others.

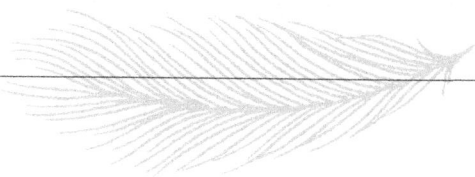

July 25th

"Every sunrise brings the promise of a new beginning; seize it with open arms."

- Greet each new day with excitement and readiness to embrace new opportunities.

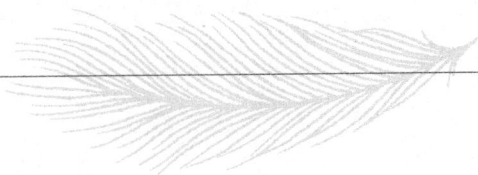

July 26th

"The beauty of life lies in embracing its imperfections with grace."

- Embrace imperfections, for they add depth and beauty to the tapestry of life.

July 27th

"In the pursuit of greatness, resilience is the oxygen that keeps you going."

- Resilience is the key to enduring and thriving through the trials and tribulations of striving for greatness.

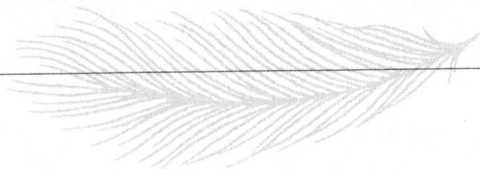

July 28th

"Your scars are reminders of your strength, not signs of weakness."

- Embrace your scars, whether physical or emotional, for they symbolize your ability to overcome and heal.

July 29th

"The ripple of kindness you create today can become a tidal wave of change tomorrow."

- Small acts of kindness can lead to significant positive impact over time.

July 30th

"Your life story is a masterpiece; paint it with colours of joy and passion."

- We have the power to shape our life's narrative with joyful and passionate experiences.

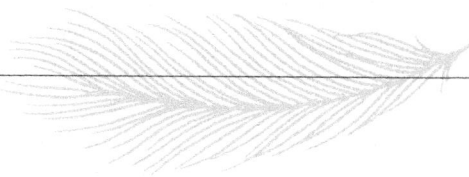

July 31st

"In the mirror of self-love, you'll find the reflection of true happiness In the mirror of self-love, you'll find the reflection of true happiness."

- Loving yourself is the foundation for cultivating a fulfilling and joyous life.

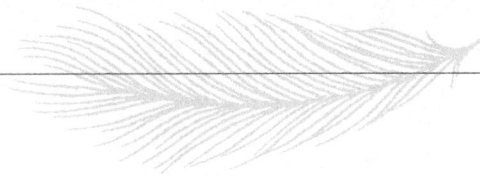

August 1st

"In the storm of adversity, hope is the guiding star that leads you home."

- Hope provides the anchor and direction during challenging times.

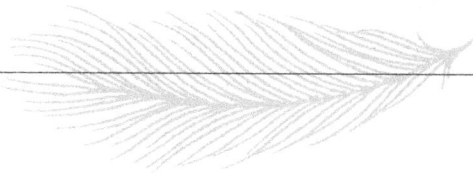

August 2nd

"In the garden of life, perseverance is the gardener of dreams."

- Perseverance nurtures and sustains the growth of our dreams.

August 3rd

"The greatest adventure in life is to discover your true self."

- Self-discovery is a lifelong journey that leads to understanding and embracing our authentic selves, unlocking endless possibilities for personal growth.

August 4th

"Embrace change, for it is the catalyst for personal evolution."

- Change may be daunting, but it also paves the way for personal growth and transformation, leading us towards new horizons.

August 5th

"Gratitude unlocks the door to abundance,
welcoming blessings into your life."

- A grateful heart attracts more blessings
and positive experiences.

August 6th

"Kindness is the universal language that transcends all barriers."

- Acts of kindness have the power to bridge gaps between cultures, beliefs, and backgrounds, fostering a sense of unity among humanity.

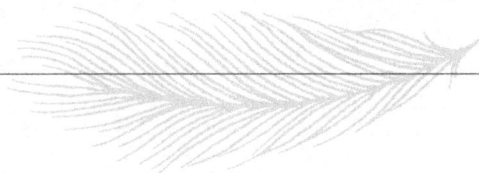

August 7th

"Believe in your dreams, even when no one else does; your belief will make them real."

- Having unwavering faith in our dreams sets the stage for their manifestation, regardless of external doubt.

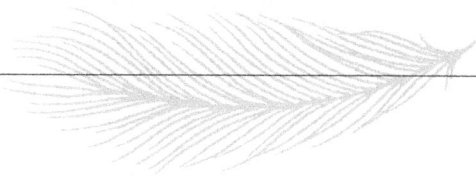

August 8th

"The only limits that exist are the ones you place upon yourself."

- Break free from self-imposed limitations, and you'll realize the boundless potential within you.

August 9th

"Embrace the rainbows in your storms, for they bring hope and beauty."

- Even amidst difficult times, there are moments of beauty and hope to be found.

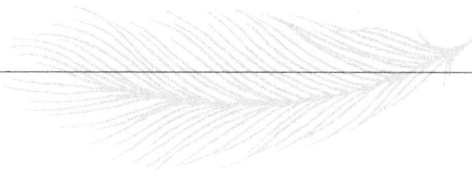

August 10th

"Empathy is the bridge that connects hearts and transforms communities."

- Empathy fosters understanding and compassion, strengthening the bonds between people.

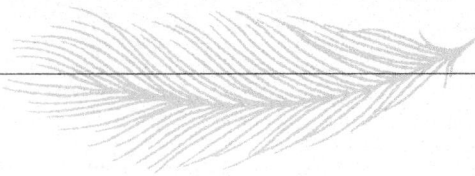

August 11th

"You hold the pen; write your life story with courage and purpose."

- Take charge of your life and create a narrative that reflects your aspirations and values.

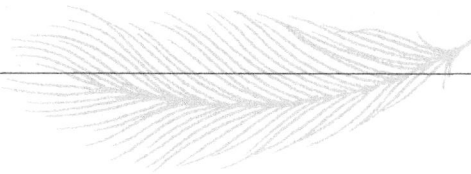

August 12th

"Within the depths of uncertainty lies the treasure of self-discovery."

- Embrace uncertainty as an opportunity for growth and self-awareness.

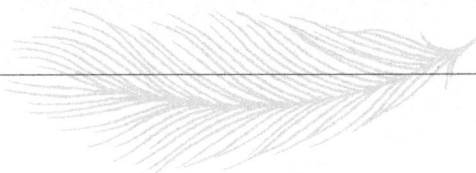

August 13th

"Your potential is like a seed; nurture it with passion, and watch it bloom into greatness."

- Just as a seed needs care and attention to grow into a mighty tree, so does our potential. Cultivate your talents with passion and dedication, allowing them to flourish into something extraordinary.

August 14th

"Plant seeds of positivity and your will harvest a garden of happiness."

- The energy we put into the world comes back to us. By spreading positivity and kindness, we create a ripple effect of joy that eventually finds its way back into our own lives.

August 15th

"Success is not measured by possessions but by the impact you leave on hearts."

- True success is not solely about material wealth but rather the positive influence and love we leave in the lives of others.

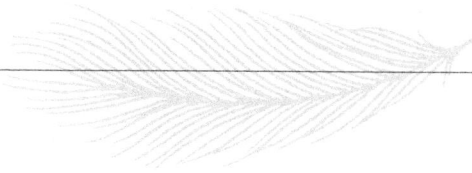

August 16th

"Choose resilience over resignation, and you'll soar above challenges."

- Resilience empowers us to face setbacks with determination, propelling us to overcome obstacles and reach new heights.

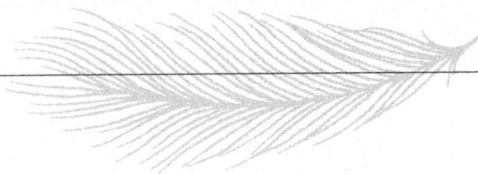

August 17th

"The true essence of beauty lies in the radiance of a kind heart."

- Kindness illuminates the soul and makes a person truly beautiful.

August 18th

"In the realm of dreams, courage is the brush that paints the canvas of success."

- Courageous actions are what turn dreams into reality and create success.

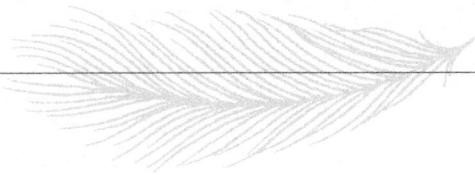

August 19th

"Believe in yourself, for your belief is the spark that ignites success."

- Self-belief fuels determination and perseverance, propelling you toward your goal and dreams.

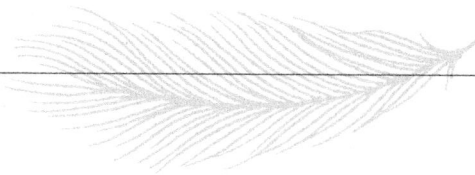

August 20th

"Gratitude is the gateway to abundance and contentment."

- Cultivating a grateful heart opens the door to recognizing and appreciating the abundance in our lives.

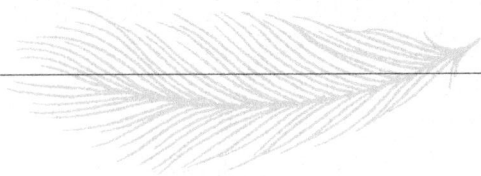

August 21st

"Your strengths are the foundation upon which greatness is built."

- Identify and harness your strengths, as they hold the power to unlock your true potential.

August 22nd

"In the realm of dreams, perseverance is the architect of destiny."

- Perseverance designs the path towards the fulfilment of our dreams.

August 23rd

"The best version of yourself exists just beyond your comfort zone."

- Growth and self-discovery happen when we step outside our comfort zones.

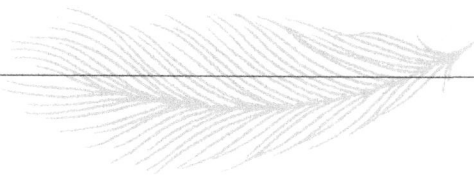

August 24th

"The universe whispers its secrets to those who listen with an open heart."

- Listen attentively to the whispers of the universe, for it reveals profound truths.

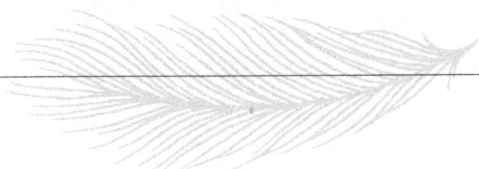

August 25th

"Let kindness be the currency that enriches your interactions with others."

- Interact with others in kindness, for it enriches the lives of both giver and receiver.

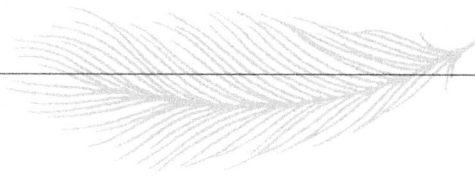

August 26th

"Every sunset is a reminder that endings can be as beautiful as beginnings."

- The end of one chapter signifies the start of another, and each moment, even the closing ones, holds its own beauty and significance.

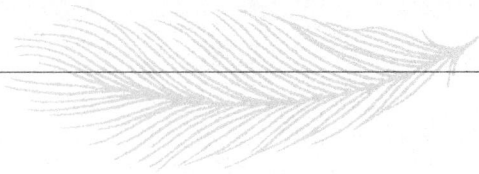

August 27th

"Happiness is not a destination; it's a way of traveling through life."

- True happiness is found in the journey itself, appreciating the little moments and cherishing every step of the way.

August 28th

"Your inner light shines brightest when you embrace your authentic self."

- Embrace your authenticity, for it is what radiates your unique brilliance..

August 29th

"Success is not a destination but an ever-evolving journey of self-discovery."

- Success is not a static point in time but an ongoing process of learning, growing, and evolving as individuals.

August 30th

"Embrace the uncertainty of life, for therein lies the magic of possibility."

- Embracing uncertainty opens us up to unforeseen opportunities and allows us to experience the wonder of life.

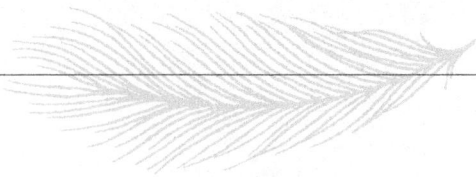

August 31st

"To inspire others, live your truth unapologetically."

- By authentically living your truth, you inspire others to do the same and create a ripple effect of courage.

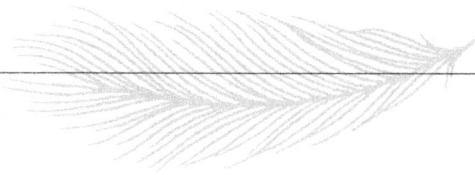

September 1st

"In the book of life, every chapter tells a story of resilience and triumph."

- Each chapter of our lives contributes to the beautiful story of our resilience and victories..

September 2nd

"Wisdom is not just in knowing but in the willingness to learn."

- True wisdom comes from recognizing that learning is a lifelong journey.

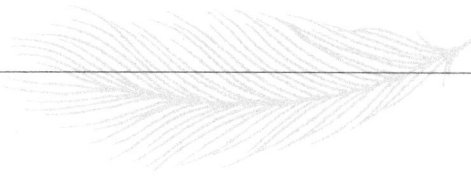

September 3rd

"In the realm of dreams, ambition is the architect of greatness."

- Ambition provides the blueprint for turning dreams into tangible achievements.

September 4th

"The power of self-belief makes the impossible merely improbable."

- Believing in yourself expands your perceived possibilities and potential.

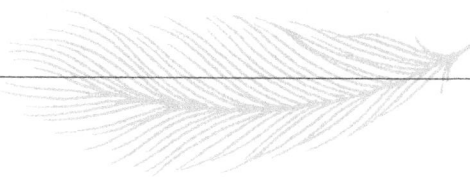

September 5th

"The journey of a thousand miles begins with a single step; take that step fearlessly."

- Starting a new venture or pursuing a dream may seem daunting, but it all starts with that first courageous step. We are reminded that even the most significant accomplishments begin with a single act of bravery.

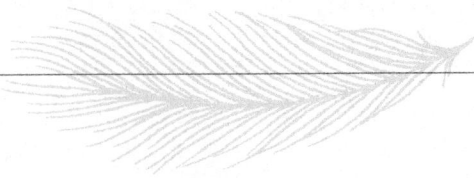

September 6th

"Practice self-care as a daily ritual. Nurture your well-being in mind, body, and spirit."

- Self-care is a daily ritual that nurtures our well-being on all levels. By prioritizing self-care in mind, body, and spirit, we replenish our energy, reduce stress, and create a foundation for holistic growth.

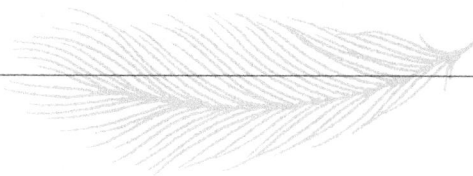

September 7th

"Your voice has the power to inspire change;
speak up and let it be heard."

- Our voices can be catalysts for change
  and progress. Use your voice for good,
  advocating for what we believe in and
  making a difference in the world.

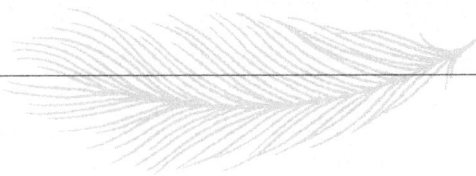

September 8th

"The journey to greatness begins with a single step of courage."

- Taking that first brave step is often the hardest, but it sets us on the path to achieving greatness.

September 9th

"Your dreams are the seeds that grow into the forests of possibility."

- Nourish your dreams, and they will flourish into extraordinary opportunities.

September 10th

"Your purpose is the compass that directs the course of your life."

- Find purpose in life, as it provides direction and clarity on your journey.

September 11th

"Your struggles are the chisel that carves your character."

- Adversities and challenges shape our resilience and reveal our true inner strength. Embrace them as opportunities for personal growth.

September 12th

"The smallest acts of kindness can create ripples of positive change."

- Never underestimate the impact of a small act of kindness; it can create a chain reaction of goodness.

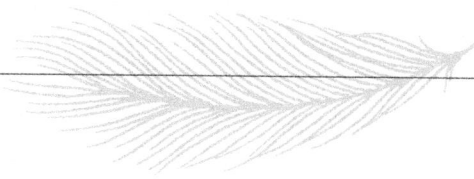

September 13th

"Success is not a destination but a continuous evolution of self."

- Success is an ongoing journey of growth and self-improvement, not a fixed endpoint.

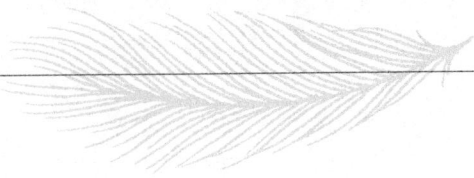

September 14th

"Life is a masterpiece; you hold the brush; paint it with colours of love and purpose."

- We have the power to shape our lives with our actions and decisions, creating a masterpiece filled with love and meaning.

September 15th

"The road to success is paved with hard work and a willingness to learn from failure."

- Embrace failures as learning experiences, and they become stepping stones to success.

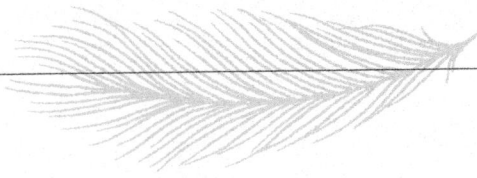

September 16th

"The symphony of life harmonizes when love is the conductor."

- Love brings harmony and connection to the various facets of life.

September 17th

"The more you give, the richer you become
in the currency of kindness."

- Generosity and kindness enrich our lives
and the lives of those around us, creating
a sense of abundance.

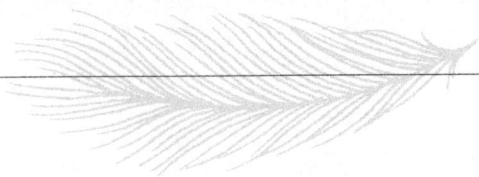

September 18th

"Your worth is not defined by others' opinions; it is found within yourself."

- Our self-worth should not be reliant on external validation but should come from recognizing our inherent value and worthiness.

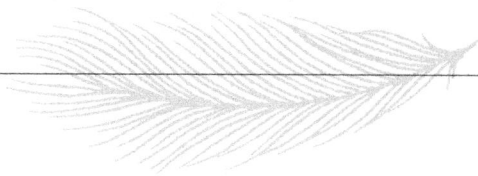

September 19th

"You are the author of your story; write it with courage and authenticity."

- We have the power to shape our lives and narratives, making choices that align with our values and passions.

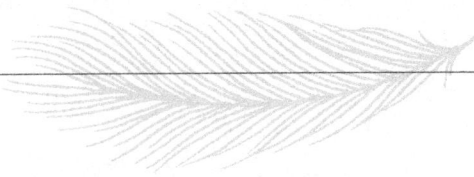

September 20th

"Success is not about the destination but the person you become on the journey."

- The growth and transformation experienced during the pursuit of success are what truly matter.

September 21st

"The power of gratitude can turn the ordinary into the extraordinary."

- Cultivating gratitude allows us to find beauty and joy in the simplest things, transforming our perspective on life.

September 22nd

"The fire within you can illuminate the world if you let it burn bright".

- Embrace your passions and talents, for they have the power to inspire and ignite positive change in the world

September 23rd

"In the pursuit of knowledge, curiosity is the compass that guides you."

- Embrace curiosity and the desire to learn, for it leads to endless possibilities and growth.

September 24th

"The power to change your life lies in your hands; it's time to start creating."

- Take ownership of your life and start actively shaping the future you desire.

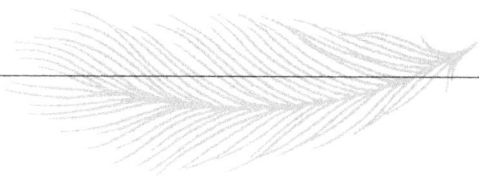

September 25th

"Celebrate your progress; it's a testament to your resilience."

- Acknowledge and celebrate each step forward, for it signifies your strength and perseverance.

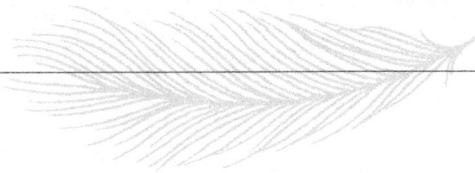

September 26th

"The tapestry of life is woven with threads of love and compassion."

- Love and compassion form the fabric that binds us all together.

September 27th

"Challenges are the brushstrokes that paint the masterpiece of resilience."

- Challenges contribute to the intricate and beautiful masterpiece of our resilience.

September 28th

"Dance to the rhythm of your own heartbeat, for that is where true joy resides."

- Authentic happiness comes from living in alignment with our values and passions. Embrace your uniqueness and follow your heart, finding fulfilment in the rhythm of your own life.

September 29th

"Embrace change fearlessly, for it carries the promise of growth and renewal."

- Change is inevitable, and embracing it allows us to evolve and reach new heights

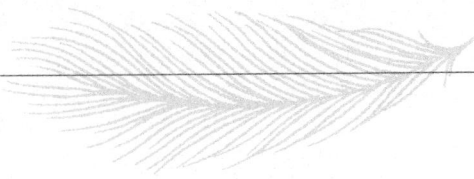

September 30th

"Kindness costs nothing but enriches
everything it touches."

- Acts of kindness have immeasurable
value and can create a ripple effect of
positivity in the world.

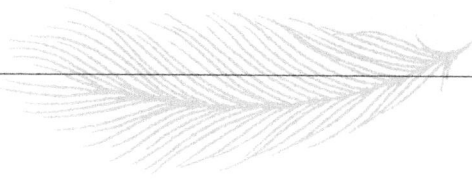

October 1st

"The key to success lies in the ability to adapt and thrive amid change."

- Embrace change and remain adaptable, for it is in the face of uncertainty that we find opportunities for growth and success.

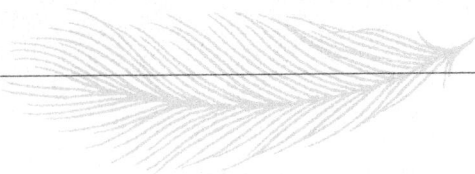

October 2nd

"The symphony of life is composed of moments, both big and small."

- Each moment contributes to the beautiful symphony of life's experiences.

October 3rd

"Your scars do not define you; they are a testament to your courage and healing."

- Scars represent healing and strength, reminding us of the battles we've fought and conquered.

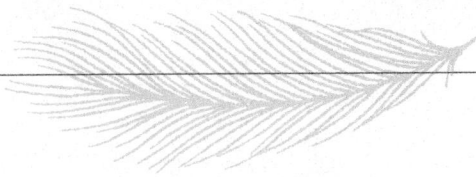

October 4th

"Embrace uncertainty; it's the canvas of possibility."

- Embracing uncertainty allows us to step into the unknown and explore new opportunities and growth. It is where creativity and innovation thrive.

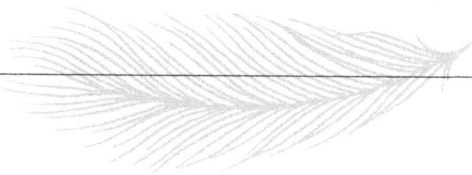

October 5th

"Dare to be different; your uniqueness is your superpower."

- Embrace your individuality and let it shine, for it is what sets you apart and makes you extraordinary.

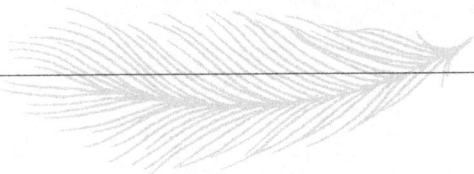

October 6th

"You are the author of your story; dare to write an extraordinary tale."

- Take charge of your life and create a narrative filled with purpose, adventure, and growth.

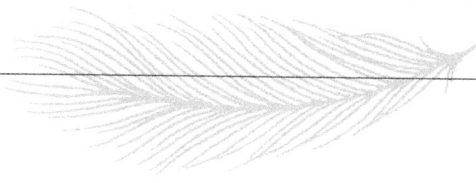

October 7th

"Trust the journey, for it leads you to where you need to be."

- Trusting the process of life allows us to let go of unnecessary worries and find solace in the unfolding of events.

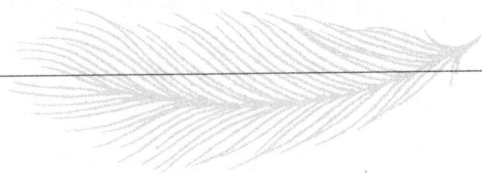

October 8th

"Find strength in vulnerability, for it is the birthplace of authenticity."

- Embracing vulnerability allows us to show our true selves and connect deeply with others.

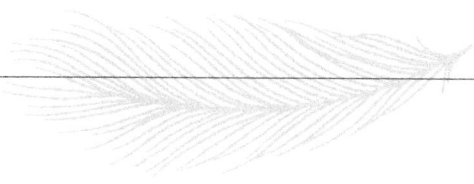

October 9th

"Your potential is limitless; don't let fear set imaginary boundaries."

- Fear can hold us back from realizing our full potential; breaking free from it opens doors to endless possibilities.

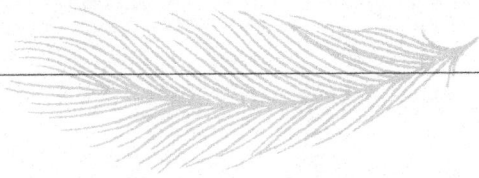

October 10th

"Kindness is the currency that enriches the soul and touches the hearts of many."

- Acts of kindness carry immeasurable value, creating a ripple effect that positively impacts countless lives.

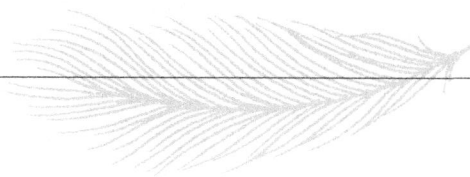

October 11th

"Patience and persistence are the keys that unlock the door to greatness."

- Achieving greatness often requires time and effort. With patience and persistent effort, we can unlock our full potential and achieve extraordinary things.

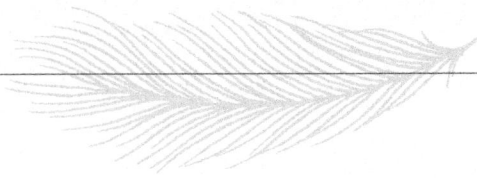

October 12th

"Life's challenges are the canvas for your resilience and creativity."

- When faced with difficulties, we have the opportunity to showcase our strength and resourcefulness, turning challenges into opportunities for growth.

October 13th

"The strength of your character is revealed in times of adversity."

- Adversity tests our character, revealing our true strength and resilience.

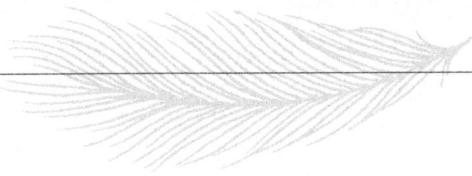

October 14th

"Let go of regrets, for they weigh down the wings of your potential."

- Dwelling on past mistakes inhibits growth, but by releasing regrets, we free ourselves to soar and embrace new possibilities.

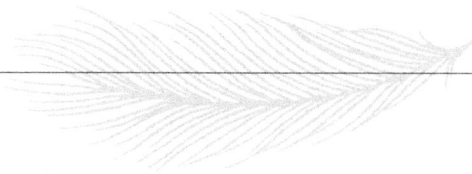

October 15th

"Success is not about how fast you reach the top, but how you help others climb alongside you."

- True success involves lifting others as we ascend, creating a supportive community that collectively achieves greatness.

October 16th

"Your story is the masterpiece you paint with the colours of your experiences."

- Our life experiences shape our unique stories, creating a masterpiece that is entirely our own.

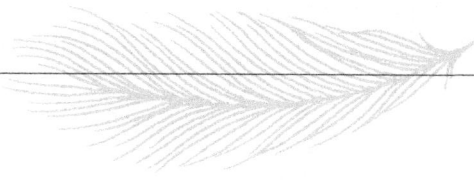

October 17th

"In the garden of success, failure is the fertilizer for growth."

- Failure provides valuable lessons that nourish personal growth and development.

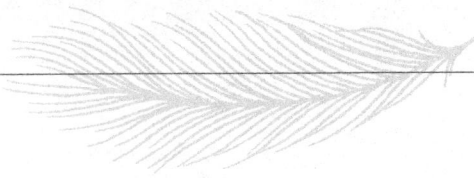

October 18th

"Nurture your inner child; it holds the secrets to unbridled joy."

- Embrace the playfulness and wonder of your inner child to experience true happiness.

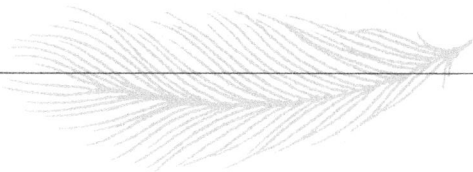

October 19th

"Your smile is a powerful healer; share it generously."

- A smile has the power to uplift spirits and bring healing to those around you.

October 20th

"Your light shines brightest when you empower others to shine too."

- Elevating others and supporting their growth amplifies the light within us all.

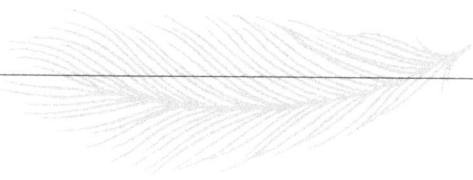

October 21st

"Your limitations are illusions that vanish when you believe in your infinite potential."

- Our beliefs shape our reality, and by breaking free from self-imposed limitations, we unlock the vast possibilities that reside within us. Be inspired to have unwavering faith in your abilities.

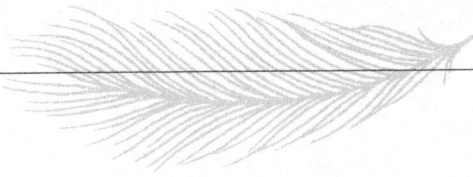

October 22nd

"The seeds of success lie in the soil of
dedication and hard work."

- Success is a product of consistent effort and
commitment to our goals

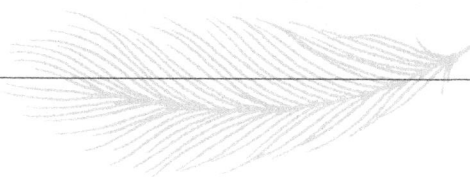

October 23rd

"When you walk with purpose, you will find the path to fulfilment."

- Having a clear sense of purpose gives direction and meaning to our lives, leading us toward fulfilled and contented existence.

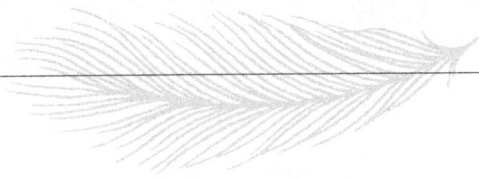

October 24th

"Embrace the dance of patience and persistence; it leads to extraordinary outcomes."

- Combining patience with unwavering persistence empowers us to achieve remarkable results over time.

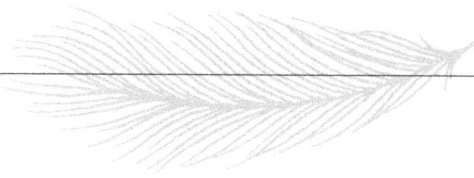

October 25th

"Within the silence of reflection, you'll discover the wisdom of the soul."

- Quiet introspection allows us to connect with our inner wisdom and intuition.

October 26th

"No one's journey is identical, so never compare your chapter to someone else's book."

- Each person's life unfolds uniquely, making comparisons irrelevant. Instead, focus on your own growth and progress.

October 27th

"With every failure, you grow stronger wings to soar to greater heights".

- Failure is not a setback but an opportunity for growth and development, preparing us for greater achievements in the future

October 28th

"Happiness is not a destination but a way of traveling through life."

- Happiness is a state of mind and can be found in the simple moments of everyday life.

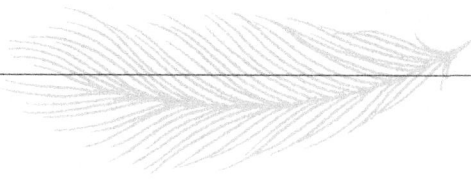

October 29th

"Let gratitude be your compass, guiding you to a fulfilled life."

- Gratitude directs us towards recognizing the blessings in our lives and fosters contentment.

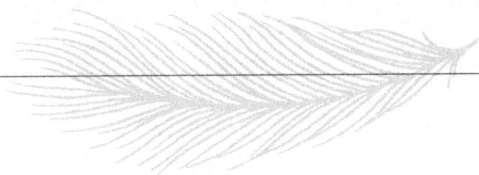

October 30th

"The key to happiness lies in embracing simplicity and finding joy in the little things."

- True happiness is often found in the simplicity of life, appreciating the beauty in everyday moments.

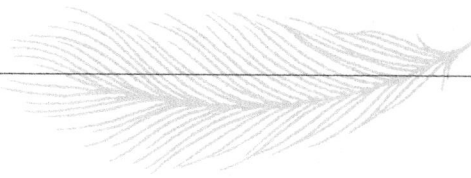

October 31st

"In the garden of dreams, perseverance
waters the seeds of success."

- Perseverance is the essential ingredient in
nurturing dreams to fruition.

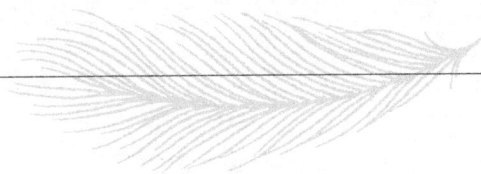

November 1st

"Empathy is the bridge that connects hearts and fosters understanding."

- Cultivating empathy enables us to relate to others' experiences and emotions, fostering a deeper connection and harmony in our relationships.

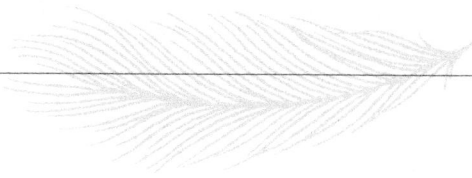

November 2nd

"The sun shines on everyone; so does the opportunity to make a difference."

- Opportunities to create positive change are available to all; we only need to recognize and seize them.

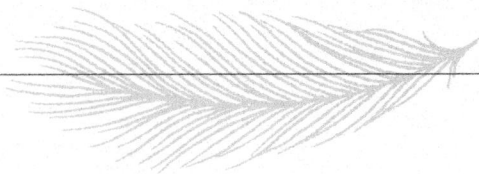

November 3rd

"The power of a kind word can spark a fire of inspiration in someone's heart."

- Simple acts of kindness and encouragement can have a profound impact on others, igniting a positive change in their lives.

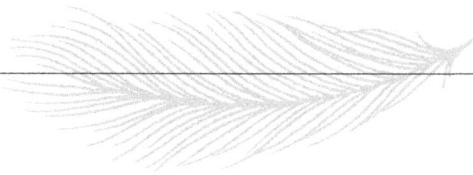

November 4h

"Choose love over fear, and watch the world transform before your eyes."

- Embracing love and compassion over fear and judgment can bring about positive change and foster harmony among individuals and communities.

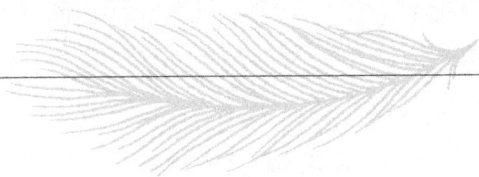

November 5th

"In the dance of time, each moment is a gift to be treasured."

- Cherish every moment, for time is our most precious resource.

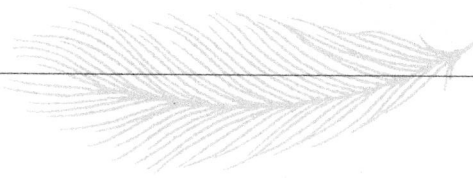

November 6th

"Rise above the storms of life and seek the rainbow that follows."

- During difficult times, maintaining a positive outlook can lead us to brighter days and better opportunities.

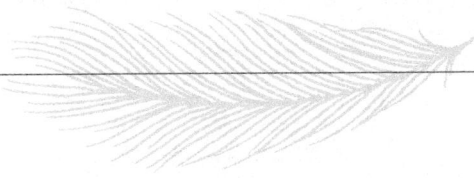

November 7th

"Every person you meet has a lesson to offer; be open to learning from everyone."

- Embracing the diversity of experiences and perspectives around us enriches our lives and broadens our understanding of the world

November 8th

"Believe in the magic of beginnings; every moment holds potential."

- Each moment is an opportunity to start anew and create something remarkable.

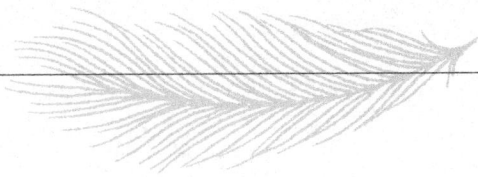

November 9th

"Believe in the beauty of your dreams, for they hold the potential to change the world."

- Our dreams can be catalysts for positive change and impact on a global scale.

November 10th

"Your presence matters; you have the power to impact lives with kindness."

- The way we show up in the world can make a meaningful difference in the lives of others.

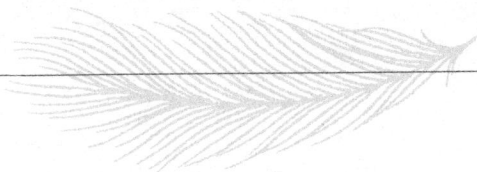

November 11th

"Courage is the force that breaks the chains
of self-doubt."

- Courage empowers us to break free from
the limitations we impose on ourselves.

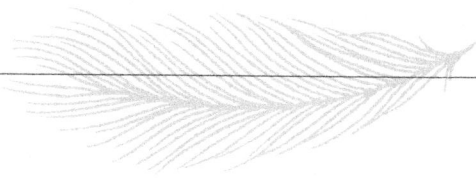

November 12th

"In the tapestry of life, gratitude weaves the threads of joy."

- Gratitude enhances our capacity for joy and appreciation of life's blessings

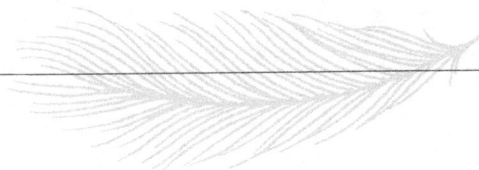

November 13th

"Embrace failure as a stepping stone, not a stumbling block, on your path to success ."

- Failure is not the end but rather a critical part of the journey. By reframing how we view failure and using it as a stepping stone to success, we foster a growth mindset and perseverance in the face of challenges.

November 14th

"Your smile is the spark that ignites joy in others' hearts."

- A simple smile has the power to brighten someone's day and create a positive ripple effect.

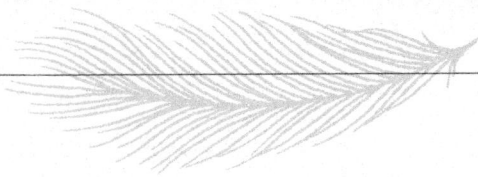

November 15th

"Believe in the powers of resilience, for it turns stumbling blocks into stepping stones."

- Resilience allows us to overcome obstacles and transform challenges into opportunities for growth and progress.

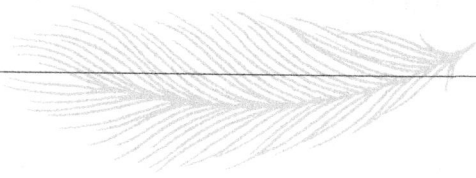

November 16th

"Fear may knock on your door, but courage invites it in for tea."

- Acknowledge fear, but let courage lead the way in facing life's challenges.

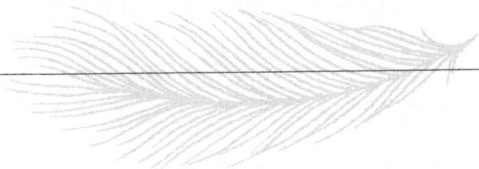

November 17th

"The strength to endure lies in the power of hope and perseverance."

- Hope and perseverance provide the stamina needed to endure life's challenges.

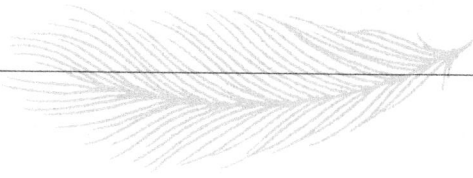

November 18th

"Your passions are the guiding stars that lead you towards fulfilment."

- Follow your passions, for they illuminate the path to a meaningful life.

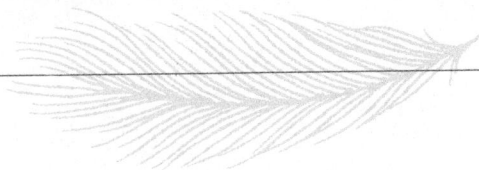

November 19th

"Plant seeds of positivity, and you will harvest a garden of happiness."

- The energy we put into the world comes back to us. By spreading positivity and kindness, we create a ripple effect of joy that eventually finds its way back into our lives.

November 20th

"Your purpose lies where your passions and the world's needs intersect."

- Discover your purpose by aligning what you love with how you can make a positive impact on the world.

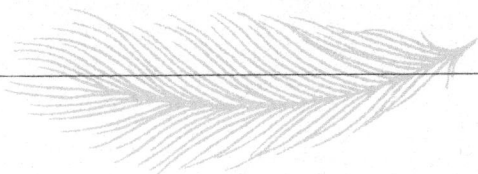

November 21st

"When you find joy in giving, you unlock the secret to abundance."

- The act of giving selflessly brings forth a sense of fulfilment and attracts abundance in various forms.

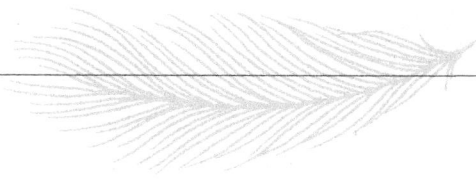

November 22nd

"With every failure, you grow stronger wings to soar to greater heights."

- Failure is not a setback but an opportunity for growth and development, preparing us for greater achievements in the future.

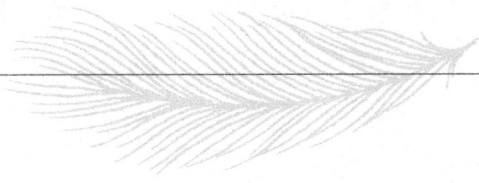

November 23rd

"Your attitude determines the altitude of your achievements."

- A positive attitude empowers you to rise above challenges and reach new heights.

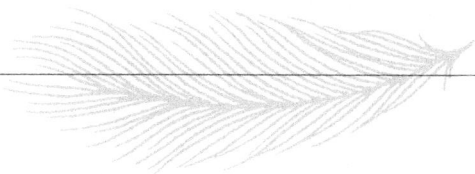

November 24th

"In the realm of dreams, courage is the architect of destiny."

- Courage designs the path towards the fulfilment of our dreams.

November 25th

"Your scars tell a story of resilience and strength; wear them proudly."

- Our scars represent the battles we've fought and conquered, a testament to our resilience and ability to overcome adversity.

November 26th

"In the face of adversity, find the strength within to conquer your challenges."

- When life throws obstacles our way, tapping into our inner strength and courage allows us to overcome any adversity that comes our way.

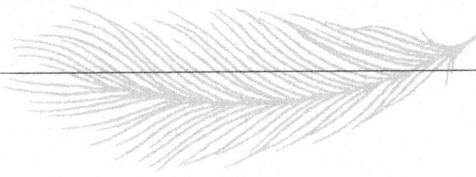

November 27th

"Success is not defined by what you have, but by who you have become."

- True success lies in personal growth, character development, and making a positive impact on the lives of others.

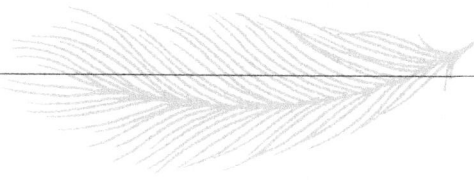

November 28th

"The path to wisdom is paved with the humility to learn from others."

- Embrace a humble attitude, as there is wisdom to be gained from every person we encounter.

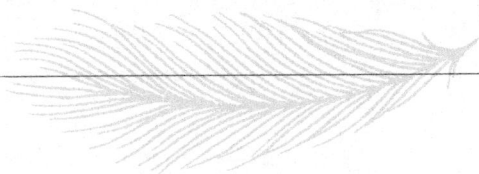

November 29th

"The journey to success begins with taking the first step, no matter how small."

- Starting is often the most challenging part, but taking that initial step sets us on the path to progress and achievement.

November 30th

"The greatest teacher lies within; listen to your heart's whispers."

- Trusting our intuition and inner wisdom can guide us towards decisions that align with our authentic selves.

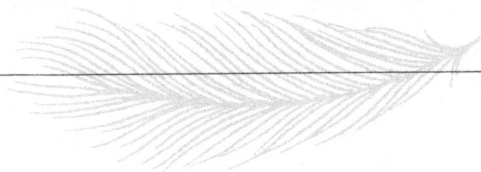

December 1st

"Forgiveness liberates you from the shackles of the past."

- Forgiving others and ourselves allows us to move forward and embrace a lighter, freer existence.

December 2nd

"The magic of life unfolds when you embrace the present moment."

- Living in the present moment allows us to fully experience the beauty of life.

December 3rd

"In the realm of dreams, courage is the key to unlocking the extraordinary."

- Dare to dream big and summon the courage to pursue those dreams fearlessly.

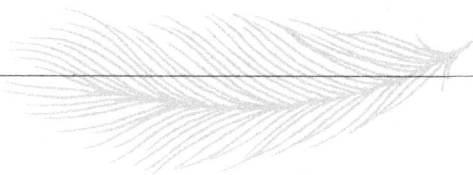

December 4th

"In the dance of life, every step forward is a celebration of progress."

- Celebrate each step forward, no matter how small, as it signifies progress.

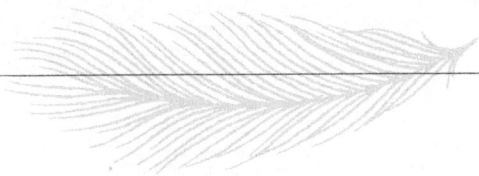

December 5th

"Believe in the symphony of your dreams;
it's time to take centre stage."

- Have confidence in your dreams, as they
deserve to be pursued with determination.

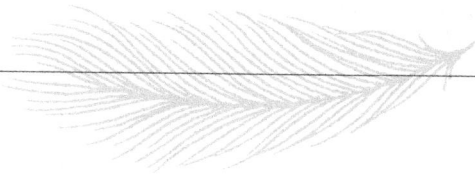

December 6th

"In the tapestry of life, every thread, even the darkest ones, weaves beauty and purpose."

- Life is a mixture of joy and sorrow, success and failure. Experience, whether positive or negative, contributes to the rich tapestry of our lives, adding depth and meaning to our journey.

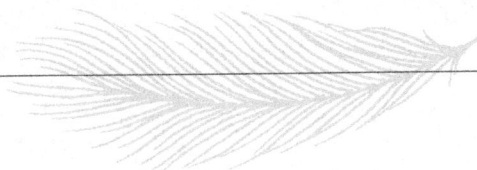

December 7th

"Wisdom is the art of learning from both success and failure."

- Embracing the lessons from all experiences, both positive and negative, enriches our understanding and wisdom.

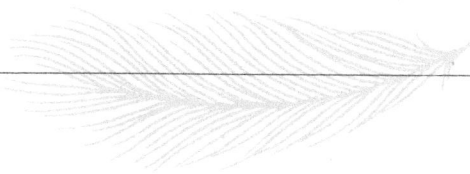

December 8th

"The strongest bonds are forged in the fires of shared experiences and unwavering support."

- Meaningful connections are built through shared experiences and supporting one another during both good and challenging times.

December 9th

"Your smile is a gift; share it generously with the world."

- A simple smile can brighten someone's day and create a positive ripple effect.

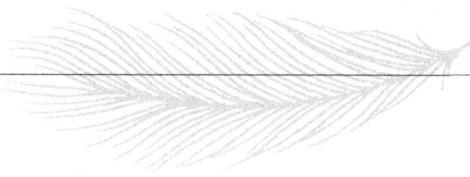

December 10th

"Every act of compassion is a seed sown to foster a kinder world."

- Each act of compassion contributes to a collective movement towards a more compassionate world.

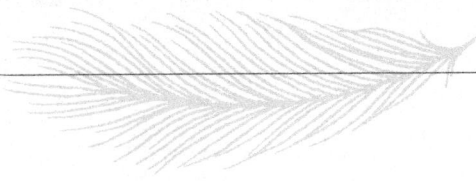

December 11th

"Success is not about the applause but the impact you leave behind."

- The true measure of success is the positive influence we have on others and the world.

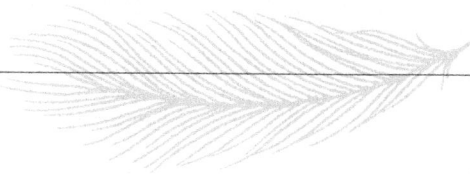

December 12th

"Your past does not define you; it merely shapes the strength within you."

- Our past experiences, whether good or bad, contribute to our resilience and fortitude. We have the power to shape our future, regardless of the challenges we've faced.

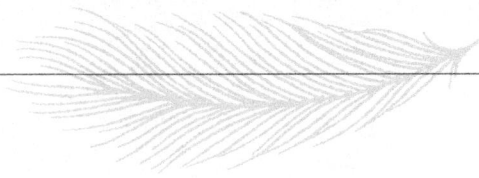

December 13th

"Find joy in the process, and success will be a natural by product."

- Focusing on enjoying the journey rather than solely fixating on the end result leads to more fulfilling accomplishments.

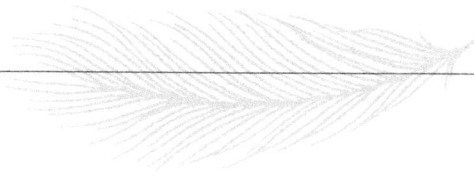

December 14th

"Success lies not in perfection, but in the courage to embrace imperfection."

- Embrace imperfections and mistakes as valuable lessons on the path to success.

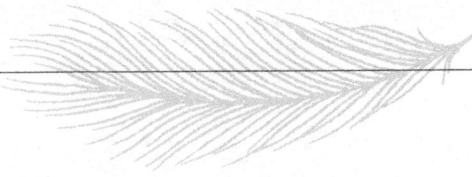

December 15th

"In the dance of destiny, every step is a manifestation of your choices."

- Our choices guide the path we tread, shaping our destiny.

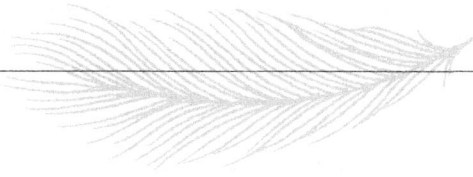

December 16th

"Happiness is not a possession; it's a state of being."

- True happiness comes from within and is not dependent on external circumstances.

December 17th

"Success is the art of turning setbacks into stepping stones."

- Transforming setbacks into opportunities for growth is the essence of success.

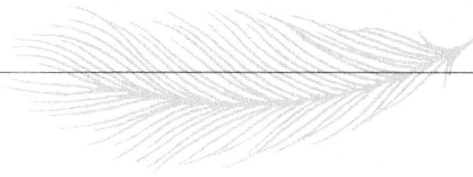

December 18th

"Within the dance of destiny, every step is a manifestation of your choices."

- Our choices guide the path we tread, shaping our destiny.

December 19th

"Believe in the beauty of your dreams, and they will become your reality."

- By having faith in our aspirations, we set ourselves on a path of determination and resilience, eventually transforming dreams into tangible achievements.

December 20th

"Be the beacon of light that guides others through the darkest storms."

- By demonstrating compassion and empathy, we can positively influence those around us and be a source of hope during challenging times.

December 21st

"Your success story starts with believing in the power of your dreams."

- Belief in your dreams is the first step towards turning them into reality.

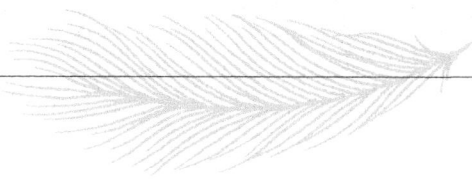

December 22nd

"Success is not measured by material wealth, but by the impact you make on others' lives."

- True success is about making a positive difference in the lives of others, leaving a lasting legacy of kindness and compassion.

December 23rd

"Don't wait for opportunities; create them with the power of your imagination."

- A creative mind can manifest countless opportunities and solutions, driving us toward our desired outcomes.

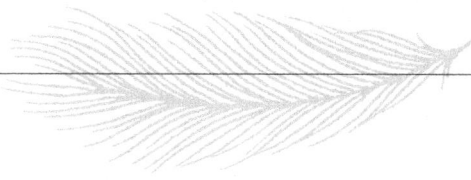

December 24th

"Find solace in nature; it holds the wisdom of life's cycles."

- Nature teaches us about change, resilience, and the beauty of impermanence..

December 25th

"Kindness is a language understood by all and spoken by the heart."

- Acts of kindness transcend cultural and linguistic barriers, connecting us all.

December 26th

"Challenges are stepping stones to triumph; keep moving forward".

- Embrace challenges as opportunities for growth, and each step forward leads you closer to victory.

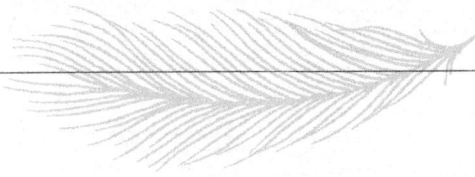

December 27th

"The universe conspires to support those who believe in their dreams."

- The universe aligns with the dreams of those who wholeheartedly believe in their potential.

December 28th

"The music of your heart can resonate with the souls of others."

- When we express ourselves authentically, our emotions and creativity connect with others on a deeper level.

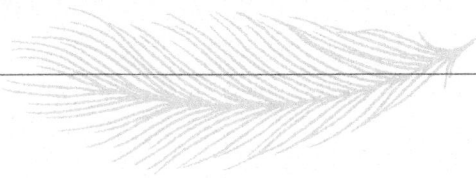

December 29th

"The world is a canvas; your actions, the brushstrokes. Paint a masterpiece of kindness and compassion."

- Recognise your power to make a positive impact in the world. Through acts of kindness and compassion, we can create a beautiful masterpiece that brightens the lives of those around us.

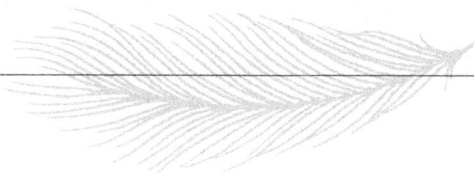

December 30th

"In the depths of darkness, the stars of hope shine brightest."

- During challenging times, hope serves as a guiding light, providing comfort and optimism.

December 31st

"Unlock the potential of every moment, for they are the building blocks of your destiny."

- Each moment contributes tour life's story. Embracing each opportunity and making the most of it shapes our future.

These quotes and explanations aim to inspire personal growth and mindfulness, reminding us of the importance of self-acceptance, gratitude, vulnerability, resilience, and embracing change. May they serve as daily reminders to cultivate a mindset of growth and live a more conscious and fulfilling life.

I hope you've enjoyed the read and have taken something positive from the words and sentiments.

There will be more books to follow.

For more information subscribe and follow me on:

Facebook
Twitter
TikTok
Instagram
Threads

DRAGONISH

Printed in Dunstable, United Kingdom

69153138R00211